LUMINA

SARAH·LAWRENCE·COLLEGE

2012
VOLUME XI

Lumina (ISSN 1539-5855) is published once yearly in April.
All correspondence should be addressed to:

Lumina
Sarah Lawrence College
Slonim House
One Mead Way
Bronxville, New York 10708

lumina@gm.slc.edu
www.luminajournal.com

Cover photo: Laurel Nakadate. From the series *365 Days: A Catalogue of Tears*, 2011. "February 19, 2010." Type C print, 50 x 40 inches.

♲ Printed on recycled paper

LUMINA 2012

EDITOR-IN-CHIEF	Molly Rose Quinn
CREATIVE DIRECTOR	Lauren Wallach
MANAGING EDITOR	Catherine Hull
EDITORIAL ASSISTANT	Michelle Campagna
SENIOR FICTION EDITOR	T Kira Madden
ASSISTANT FICTION EDITOR	Leah Schnelbach
SENIOR NONFICTION EDITORS	Brittany Baker Kendra Rajchel
SENIOR POETRY EDITOR	Micaela Mascialino
ASSISTANT POETRY EDITOR	Sophia Starmack
CONTEST DIRECTOR	Mya Green
MARKETING DIRECTOR	Leah Schnelbach
COPY EDITORS	Carla Carlson Justine Haus Margueya Novick Sebastian Hasani Paramo Jeffrey W. Peterson Courtney L. Sexton Ursula Villarreal-Moura
ART DIRECTOR	Jonathan Bourland

CONTENTS

ARTWORK

POETRY CONTEST

CONTRIBUTORS

DEAR READER

WORKING TOWARD THE development of a book, particularly one which is authored by so many, has been an astonishing privilege. What you have in your hands is older than most anything. A book is at once organic, religious, functional. This volume was produced by a staff of 34 managers, editors, and readers. As they well know, this work is not like writing; it is not, regrettably, an evolved version of an artist before a canvas. It is that other thing. It is the daily checklist, the submission of self, the constant compromise. It is, at its center, labor: that humbling and humiliating thing.

To my classmates and coworkers: I owe you an infinite debt. You have again and again redefined volunteerism. To Lauren Wallach, Creative Director, and Catherine Hull, Managing Editor: you have shown your devotion to excellence with joy and ardency.

Laurel Nakadate, whose photograph appears on our cover, pushed me to blur the distinctions between subject and object. I only hope that a modicum of her innovation can be found in these pages. Carolyn Forché, who judged our 2012 Poetry Contest, and Dorothy Allison, who was interviewed for this issue, were selected with enormous purpose. These two women bravely allow their art to speak directly to social change. The traditions they have authored are our constant lens.

The development and production of the book you hold in your hands would not be possible without the following individuals: Susan Guma, Alba Coronel, Rebecca Linz, Alexandra Soiseth, Vijay Seshadri, Fred Baumgarten, Laura Goldberg, Julia Parris, Jill Pittman, Jonathan Bourland, and Ralph Mondesand.

I would also like to show my gratitude to those who have offered support to me personally during my tenure as Editor-in-Chief: Susan Quinn, Robert Quinn, Conor Quinn, Patrick Quinn, Laura Holzman, Cathy Park Hong, Marie Howe, Marie-Hélène Westgate, Mira Ptacin, Molly Tolsky, Daniel Long, and Erica Wagner.

Sincerely,

Molly Rose Quinn
February 3, 2012

Kimberly Grey, *Subway Beach*, 2011. Photograph.

GREYHOUND, WISCONSIN, 1989

Peter Orner

SHE STUCK HER burning cigarette between her knees and raised both hands to fix her hair. It was a remarkable gesture and she seemed to do it without thinking and he wondered if this was the first time she'd done it, or if it was something she'd practiced. They were on a short break. Soon they'd be back on the bus. It was almost dark. They were in a Hardee's parking lot, he wasn't sure what town, somewhere south of Rhinelander by now, and the cigarette burned on between her knees. When she finished with her hair, she scissored it up with two fingers and went on smoking.

The driver stood up and brushed the crumbs off his pants.

He never spoke to her. After they reached the station in Chicago, he never saw her again. On the bus he watched her. She was two rows behind him. He'd stand up and sit down again. Hours he did that. As she slept, she held her head up with one hand, her elbow in her lap. Her body moved to the shifts and sways of the bus.

What if I don't remember this?

Outside in the dark, Wisconsin, where things were still possible.

SRI PANCH RAMESH

Inara Cedrins

I write on deckle-edged paper: this is the book
of loving you, whose skin is like rosewood,
who painted my snake cabinet with the expensive varnish,
clear as water. Adonis, Narcissus. When we ride
I shift so that my shadow is on your back,
shielding you from the hot sun: I want to be
a protective canopy for you, like the one made
by seven serpent kings. From under your helmet
curl locks of shining hair, like the word you taught me
for the pattern of silk swirling in the wind,
resampiriri.

You are an anemone,
gently moving tentacles. But if I touched you
you'd close up. Play dead, perhaps.

If I died, would you mourn me for thirteen days,
a recluse, sleeping on the floor of the room
and dressed in orange, not shaving;
eating only one meal a day? I think so.
I want to be cremated,
but build a resting place to remember me,
where anyone could sleep.

A mat of straw, a clay pot, a leaf plate.

TWENTY MILES FROM WISDOM

Kathryn Wiese

OROFINO, IDAHO IS a land of sifting and sorting and throwing to the wayside. It's Idaho gold country. At least, it was. Orofino took its name from a mining town to the east called *Oro Fino* (Spanish for fine gold) that burned down in 1867 and was never rebuilt. The modern Orofino offers little more than a high school, prison, and mental hospital. A person's either free or locked-up, sane or a lunatic. Less than a mile down the road from the mental hospital is Orofino High School. Their mascot is the Maniac.

My father spent two years at Idaho State Hospital North in Orofino. In 2002, local police arrested him in his hometown of McCall, Idaho and charged him with assault against an employee at McPaws, the local dog pound. My father's dog Snoopy had run away, and in order for my father to retrieve him the employee insisted he pay a $160 recovery fee. My father became a transient mountain man after he and my mother divorced in 1991. With barely enough money to live on and a dog as his only companion, the fact that he would have to pay for Snoopy's return was understandably upsetting. The incident reports about the actual altercation itself are contradictory. Either my father shoved the female employee out of his way, or she became aggressive with him first. Both parties behaved poorly and my father was put on the police watch list. Snoopy stayed at McPaws. Less than a month later a woman overheard my father making a threat against the McPaws employee, and he was arrested. He has always made empty threats, never quite understanding why people believe them. I knew nothing of all this for the first two weeks—I was in high school across the country in New Hampshire—but during his third week in jail he sent me a letter. "Well Katie," it began, "I have some news."

Hearing after hearing got postponed and his imprisonment in the small, cement-celled county jail stretched into months. It was like watching rainwater drip-drip-drip into a bucket, then waking one morning to find the bucket full, too heavy to overturn.

After multiple trial postponements, a judge sentenced my father to two months of psychiatric monitoring at State Hospital North in Orofino. Due in part to a zealous County Prosecutor, the hospital stay that was supposed to be two months became two years. The Prosecutor saw him as a violent, mentally disturbed man who would be a threat to society. Years dripped by. Two years of dinners before the sun went down, of twin beds draped with blue cotton blankets, of three-minute phone calls next to the nurse's station, two years of captivity.

In 2010, eight years after his release, I decided I wanted to visit Orofino. I thought that going there would help me understand my father better. The last time I'd seen him was at my college graduation in 2009. He drove 600 miles from Montana to get to my graduation party, but got turned around in the neighborhoods less than a mile away from the house. He found a parking lot, called me from his cell phone, and we started walking toward one another. Five thousand feet above, the sun glowed through a layer of cumulus mounds down onto our heads.

Going to Orofino held the kind of hope for me that drew nineteenth century Americans to its humble, gold-riddled creeks. State Hospital North was a place where my father was unable to hide himself. His doctors must have gotten a more complete picture of him than I ever had. The hope itself was a valuable prospect.

Upon release from State Hospital North, my father's official diagnosis was a mixed type delusional disorder and schizotypal personality disorder. I had to Google it. Schizotypal personality disorder, the Mayo Clinic online told me, is a psychiatric condition where a person struggles with interpersonal relationships and disruption in thought and behavioral patterns. These people cling to ideas, sometimes delusions, so strongly that they're isolated from normal human relationships. My father, for example, spent ten years working on a vapor carburetor convinced it would change the state of automotives. He still takes it (a full engine) with him everywhere he goes in the backseat of his car. I struggle to understand how the diagnosis relates to him—how much of his behavior is mental illness and how much is eccentricity, or even just loneliness? Being classified mentally ill keeps my father on a monthly government stipend, but to him the check is more than money. It is a definition. He struggles against it, and has tried time and time again to get the classification removed from his record. But for now, so-called mental illness is just another load he must carry with him, another piece of broken-down machinery that he alone cannot fix.

Today, ten years after his release from Orofino, my father lives in southwestern Montana, traveling from one town to the next in his bartered-for motor home. In the summers, he sets up camp somewhere along the Beaverhead River; in winters, KOA camps with cheap electric hook-up. Whenever we talk on the phone, he reports his location. "Well, I'm about 20 miles south of Wisdom," he said once. I chuckled; he didn't. Turns out Wisdom, Montana wasn't much kinder to him than other parts of the Intermountain West—he'd run out of gas on the highway.

Within days of deciding I wanted to travel to Orofino, I spoke with an administrator at State Hospital North to arrange my visit. I asked my father to sign and notarize a waiver releasing his medical records, which he did. Since I didn't have a driver's license, I convinced a friend to drive with me from Massachusetts to Idaho. The trip came together nicely at first. I told myself the ease meant Orofino was the gold I'd been seeking since the day my father was admitted. Perhaps if I saw the mental hospital where he had been housed, I'd understand more of him—the ways he'd changed from the man who helped raise me, and the ways he hadn't. Maybe with context—other patients and barred windows and paper cups full of pills—his odd, antisocial ways would be easier to differentiate from lunacy.

I wanted to see the crafts room at the hospital. I wanted to know what medications he was given, why he was taken off them and put on others, and why he refuses to take them now. I wanted to see the gravel path that winds around the grounds, the one he was given special privileges to run on every other morning. Did he wake up to the sound of honey locust seed pods, long and slender, crunching beneath his tennis shoes? I wanted to know what kinds of trees grew at the hospital—pictures from the Chamber of Commerce online showed a heavily forested landscape—and I wanted to know how they smelled. Did the scent of ponderosa pines ever waft past his window, overpowering the detergent smell of his pillowcase in the earliest hours of the morning, so that for an instant he'd forget where he was? Or did the ponderosas haunt him? Maybe their smell reminded him of Ponderosa State Park where he used to run, where he taught me how to ride a bike. Maybe their sway, their falling needles and bark, reminded him of a life he'd left behind.

The day I was born my father was away chopping firewood in the ponderosa forest two hours north of our home in Boise. The Idaho wilderness was uncharacteristically soggy that September in 1986; twigs bent rather than snapped underfoot. But that Tuesday morning the sun shone clear and he decided to gather the winter firewood before he had a newborn. It's hard for me to remember a time with no cell phones, no text message baby alerts. But that's how it was—he was utterly unreachable—just him, a chainsaw, some gloves, and a truck with spotty radio reception. He had no way of knowing that my mother had gone into labor at work, or that I was coming three weeks ahead of schedule.

It wasn't until he got home late that night that he suspected something was amiss. It started with the chill of the house—no one had fed the wood stove—and was confirmed by the blinking red light on the answering machine. My father has told me the story so many times it almost feels like my own memory. The dog lay next to the wood stove, curled up tight to keep warm, and a cloud of moisture escaped his muzzle in a sigh. My father pulled up to the house, opened the front door, and hollered for my mother. The light shining in from the street illuminated him from behind. He glimpsed the blinking light on the answering machine and without even listening to the message he got back in the truck and drove to the hospital. There, a nurse calmly directed him to the maternity ward. He ran the whole way. He was dirty and sweaty from a long day in the woods and with every footfall his mud-caked boots shed clods of dirt on the linoleum. When he found the labor room, the first thing he saw was my mother's profile, her dark hair tucked behind her ear. Next he saw the caterpillar-like bundle in her arms, small, more blanket than baby. He reached out for the bundle, muscles aching from hauling wood all day, and as he lifted his only daughter for the first time, he nearly tossed her over his head.

"Whoa," he said, grinning and bouncing her in his hands, "she's so light!"

Even for all my longing, I never made it to Orofino. The day I received his medical records in the mail, an unassuming manila envelope wedged behind the screen door, I got a call from the friend who'd offered to drive me to Idaho. He couldn't do it, he said; there was a doctor's appointment that couldn't wait. I finally forgave him when nine months later his girlfriend gave birth to a saucer-eyed girl. My desire to visit State Hospital North, I think, was not so different from the broken-down engine my father carries in the backseat of his car: born of a desire to fix, to make right. My father is a man beyond words. I can call him a mountain man, I can call him a loner, I can even call him a schizoid—but none of those things get at the heart of him, at the man who nearly tossed me over his head in delight. It's clear that Orofino alone will not reveal that man. The town has given me the process though. It's taught me how to seek, how to sift, and how to throw the rest to the wayside.

Yumna Al-Arashi, *Yemen*, 2010. Photograph.

AGE SIX

Shevaun Brannigan

The night mother splits father's lip with the bottle, I run to the garden.
Slip through the bamboo stalks and stand in their center,
squinting at the crescent moon. Beneath my feet, a snake's
bubbled skin like wax paper, beetles shifting through the soil
like gravediggers. My parents rush to the car, the fireflies
flying in splatters of light around them to the sound of crickets
swelling, the slow cry of the screen door struggling to shut.
Later I find blood on the kitchen walls, Rorschach blots in red.
I see lungs, women with buckets, I see a yelling face with flushed cheeks.
The linoleum floor begins to shake, then crack, stalks of bamboo shoot through.
When I wake up it's father leaning over me, his mouth stitched shut
with black thread, like fishing line tangled around two skinned fish.

FUNERAL FOR CONFUSION

Hari Alluri

though he didn't cheat,
lolo never lost at cards.
he survived two wars.

in form, lola survived him.
on her deathcot, tobacco

wrinkled lips crowing
beside me in tagalog,
the closest language

she knows to english: you are
just like my husband. charming,

charmed, i once rolled a
perfect dice game. anything,
alive or else, will

answer if you feel to ask.
not blood, by marriage, my dead

uncle lingers at
being reborn as my child.
after we kill him,

he comes by in raven form,
mimics vocab from beyond

my ears' horizons,
whispers me truths, those truths my
lolo never got

to lullaby. there's that voice,
he says, by blood or marriage,

older and wiser
than you. sometimes you even
catch it inventing

spirits. under its drunken
tutelage, i touch my head

with dirt, nodding like
i understand, afraid to
hear what else it knows

CANNED

William Cordeiro

Worn belts chuckled by
all day within the pickle
factory until it buckled

under. Vinegar still wafts
through half the town
depending on the blow

of wind. The last laugh's
had by the jarring smell,
canceled men preserving

their dignity by trading
smokes and smack, box
scores, or just rubber-

necking each new muscle
car at the folded old drug
store. One offers a hand

mangled in the gears, and
stumps a bud, piping up,
holding out a last slow nub.

ARGOS

Lorna Knowles Blake

Patient-hearted hunter, neglected, flea-bitten.
Where is your Odysseus? Aged beyond knowing,
striding home, the warrior spies his loyal hound
    rising to greet him.

Vigil over, Argos, exhausted, flattens
his ears, lowers his tail and dies. Today,
watching the dog wait at the door for hours,
    I can believe it.

Where is his Odysseus? Errand or war,
it's the same to him, dumb, devoted creature.
Good dog. I say, *He'll be back.* I promise you.
    Ithaka's waiting.

Alex Manthei, *Occupy London Crowd*, 2011. Photograph.

TERROR FOR TOTS

Mary Morris

THE ELEVATOR IS broken so Emma takes the stairs. She flings her bag on her shoulder and starts her climb. Before the first landing she smells marijuana wafting from 2B, the pets whose cages need cleaning in 3F. Music cascades from the fourth floor; voices shout in languages she can't understand. She's furious that the elevator is broken again. And that faded sign taped to its door: "Moter broke, fixe tomorrow." It's been up a dozen times since she moved in. She resists the temptation to take out her pen and correct it.

On the fifth landing Jesus startles her. He's smoking a cigarette in front of his grandmother's door. He's often hanging out here when he should be in school. With his hair, buzz cut into a spider's web, and that crucifix in his ear, he's trying to look cool. He's got a man's body, but a boy's face. Eyes like a puppy in a pet store. "Whassup?" he asks as she rounds the bend.

"Not much," Emma replies, scurrying up the stairs.

She's not afraid of Jesus. But the building is a little dicey. It reminds her of a jail with its long dark corridors, its cinderblock walls. Cigarette butts and fliptops are scattered on the floor. She's seen crack vials and condoms as well. Stranger men than Jesus lurk in the corners. There's the heavyset guy with the oily smell and facial piercings, though Emma has three rings in her left ear and a silver fairy wrapped around her lobe, so who is she to judge? Still, shadows in the dim-lit corridors make her nervous.

Just before she moved into this neighborhood, a girl carrying groceries home was stabbed in the back. This put Emma's parents on red alert. Her father, who rarely crosses the Harlem River, scoured the neighborhood like a private eye and declared it unsafe. "Anything that doesn't have a golf course would be unsafe to you," Emma said.

At her landing, Emma unbolts the door. She looks over her shoulder to make sure Jesus hasn't followed her. Then dashes inside.

"Brian," she calls out. It's almost nine, and she's hoping he's home. She's hungry, but didn't pick up anything for dinner. Maybe tonight can be her birthday again or their anniversary the way it was last week. Some occasion they need to celebrate. "Hey, anybody here?"

But Brian isn't home. It's close to Thanksgiving so he's working late. It's his busiest time of year. She opens the fridge and finds two beers and half a container of blueberry yogurt. She starts planning their meal. She's been dreaming of corn fritters from Punch. Or that foie gras with caramelized onion from Union Square Café. Usually they don't hit up the same place twice. But it was so good last time.

Emma dumps a glass of water on her African violet which seems to demand it. She knows it's pointless. She can't keep a houseplant alive. She can't even remember she has a houseplant. Her doctor has explained her loss of short-term memory. The hippocampus shrinks from trauma. She laughs when he says the word "hippocampus" and pictures hippos sitting in classrooms, taking notes. Prozac helps with this problem. But she refuses treatment—as her doctor has duly noted in her chart.

Though loss of memory can't explain the dishes in her sink or the laundry piled on chairs, it might account for the wall of Post-its. It's been growing like a military campaign. A blueprint for the invasion of a small country. On hundreds of notes are the scribbles of things she needs to look up, people to contact, books to read, facts to Google, bits of information, cryptic messages, a FEMA map of New York, Mayan predictions for the end of the world, Aztec, Inca, and Nostrodamus too, a joke she doesn't want to forget, a name she must recall, apocalyptic scenarios of solar flares, moving to Mars. She buys the Post-Its at the stationery store on Flatbush. She's particular about the colors. She prefers the neon collection—chartreuse, violet, tangerine—to the usual pastels. She spends her evenings moving them around.

This is what she's doing as Brian walks in, dressed in overalls, humming one of those country-western tunes that get stuck in her head. "I can't take you to the dawg show cuz I'm afraid you'll win." It's better than "I've flushed you from the toilet of my heart." But still. Brian's got a band, a demo cd, but he walks around singing like a retard.

"Where do you hear that crap?" she asks as he gives her a kiss and heads for the shower. He throws up his hands. She can tell he's had a bad day. "What's wrong?"

"I messed with Bullwinkle." He shakes his head forlornly. When Brian isn't rehearsing with his band, he works for BOC Helium. The company that blows up the Macy's Thanksgiving Day Parade balloons. But Brian has serious left/right confusion. It's a form of brain damage, Emma's read. It was so bad that last year he had LEFT and RIGHT tattooed on the knuckles of his respective hands. He can play his guitar upside down like Hendrix, but he has trouble following inflation orders.

He can stand, baffled, before: "Lie Barney face down, facing Central Park; blow up tail; blow up right ear; left ear; right foot; left foot; right arm; left arm; slowly begin blowing up torso." Is that his right or mine, he'll wonder.

"What happened?" Emma asks, still inspecting her wall.

"I fucked up the practice drill." He tells her how he blew up Bullwinkle's right antler and right leg at the same time and the balloon turned on its side and rose through the trees as if it had just woken up and had somewhere to go.

Emma doesn't like to think of Bullwinkle, drifting away. "I'm hungry," she says, following him toward the bathroom.

"So, what's for dinner?" He's peeling off his clothes.

"Well, I was thinking..." She gives him a sly grin. "We haven't been out in a while."

From his smile she can tell he's game. "It could be my birthday."

"Naw, we did that last week."

"Anniversary?"

"That was the week before."

"Well," she looks at him coyly, "didn't you just get a new job or something?"

Brian shoots a fist into the air. "Record gig! Need to celebrate." He cocks his head of brown curls that remind her of Harpo Marx. "Okay, so what'd you have in mind, Patria? Gotham Grill?"

But Emma's having second thoughts. "You know, I'm thinking maybe avoid the city? Stay in the hood? How about the River Café? We've never been." Emma's done her homework, studying the Brooklyn Zagat. She thinks they should be more careful, not get too well-known in the city. It's best not to repeat themselves.

"Sounds great. I'll just be a sec...." As he heads into the shower, Emma returns to the wall that contains her secret weapon, her "get rich quick" scheme. It's been brewing for months. The idea came to her one day when she was browsing through a shelf of Dummy books. *Wine for Dummies. Tai Chi for Dummies.* It wasn't long after 9/11 when she learned that in the event of a dirty bomb there's really no way out of New York. For the past year she's been making notes. *Evacuation for Dummies.* And, the one she thinks will make her a lot of money, the watered-down version for children: *Terror for Tots.*

She's collected tidbits on disasters. And evacuation. Stage practice drills. Make everyone aware of site-specific elements such as stairwells and exits. Keep a handkerchief and small bottle of water in your desk drawer at all times. Moisten the handkerchief in the event of smoke. In a big building always go to the center. Never get into an elevator. Never stand near the windows and look out. Don't take the obvious route. Emma has appendices planned on homeland security and early warning signs. How to read body language on an airplane (the Department of Defense provides guidelines). Plus, useful hints such as how to get nail scissors (wrap the tips in gauze) through security.

But she's got the most hope for *Terror for Tots.* Helping children move past fear. It begins with, "Most people in the world are good but some are bad and sometimes bad people do things to good people." She knows it needs work, but it's moving along. She's tried to interest a few publishers, but they tell her they need to see more. One was very blunt. "This is a downer," the editor wrote. Emma knows about being a downer.

As a teenager she thought she'd had her share of disappointments: rained-out softball games, a tear in her toreador pants, restaurants that were out of shrimp. Her thighs didn't fit neatly into a size 6. Then her brother, Timmy, went off to the quarry alone one night. What was I thinking? she asks herself now.

Brian's taking an extra long shower, and Emma contemplates crawling into the bathroom on all fours. Licking his legs the way dogs do. She recalls fondly when they met at a bar on the Lower East Side. When he asked if he could call her, she gave him the phone number of the Rejection Hotline—a number she kept on hand. Brian dialed and got the message, "If you received this phone number, you have been rejected....You have not been given this number in error. For automated rejection support press 1, to speak with a care counselor press 2...."

Two months later she ran into him again at the same bar. "Hey," he said to her, a smile on his face, "that was funny."

"So," she smiled back, "you can take a joke."

She opens the bathroom door and is greeted by a cloud of steam. "Well, hello," Brian says. She sees his body through the glass. It is long and sleek. She stands there, looking at him. "Hey," he says, "It's cold."

Her stomach growls. "I'm hungry," she says.

"So get dressed."

Emma pulls on a pleather skirt, a sequined top, and heels. A short leather jacket. While she's waiting to use the bathroom, she checks out the website for the River Café. She can almost taste their tuna tartare. A few minutes later Brian emerges, dressed in jeans and a T-shirt. That's because he doesn't go inside. He drives the getaway car. But Emma has to look good.

She pops into the bathroom. She makes a circle in the steamed-up mirror. Her face looks like a ghost. She washes it, gives her hair a brushing. Opens her makeup bag filled with Urban Decay. She glides Dark Sniper beneath her eyes, rubs a shimmering blue Shattered across her lids. Smears Illegal across her lips. She dabs a touch of Paranoia on her cheeks and they're out the door.

It's warm for November. Almost Indian summer as Brian drives his battered Chevy and Emma navigates. That is, she points because of Brian's dyslexia. "Take a left here." She jabs her finger across his face. As they pull up to valet parking at the River Café, Emma jumps out and shoos the young man who approaches to take their car away. "I'll be right back," she says as she gives Brian a little "Reporting for Duty" salute.

She's hoping for a busy night, a nice crowd. And the maitre d' in a good mood as she goes in, stiletto heels clicking on the pavement, and makes her pitch. "Listen, my boyfriend just got a big record contract and we're out celebrating...." The maitre d' is listening in that polite

New York way where you know he's really thinking if he should reschedule his training session at the gym. "And I see you're very crowded, but he just loves your tuna tartare. He's waiting outside and I was wondering...."

The maitre d' gives her a smile. He's friendly enough, with dark wavy hair. Italian, maybe. "No problem," he says, "I'm sure we can accommodate you at the bar."

Emma thinks about this. "Oh, great." She's fiddling with the fairy ring in her ear, "I'll tell him." The bar won't do. The tuna tartare would cost thirty bucks, not including the wine. Emma goes outside and before the valet can say anything, jumps into the car. "No go," she says, "there's room at the bar."

"Okay," Brian says, "where to?"

It began accidentally really, the way most good discoveries do. A year ago on her birthday they drove by El Nino. The restaurant was packed so she asked if she could have their chocolate parfait and eat it in her car. "I've been dreaming of this dessert all year," she told them, which was true. The dessert itself was so-so, not at all what she remembered, and she tried to muster her enthusiasm when she went back to return the dish and pay. Instead they wished her a happy birthday and wouldn't take a cent.

After that they started driving around to all kinds of restaurants on special occasions—or not so special. They'd say it was a birthday, an anniversary, some commemorative event. They would only want an appetizer or a dessert, something they can still taste, though more and more it was things they'd never tried. They picked the items online. They'd sit eating in the car and invariably when they went to return the plate, the item was free.

Brian tells Emma that she has a criminal mentality. That this is a form of stealing, but Emma says not. It's a little scam, maybe, but it's not theft in any real sense. "It's not 'Dine and Dash,' after all," the latest in restaurant crime. Or "Chew and Screw" as she also thinks of it. (After your meal, say you're going out to have a cigarette, then leave). Nobody gets hurt. It's just kind of fun.

In truth Emma's not sure why she does this. She was never a klepto beyond the occasional eraser or candy bar. But at times it's as if she has to be fed in this way or not at all. "So, where to?" Brian asks, running a hand through his curls with some force—as if checking to make certain his head is still there.

"I don't know," Emma shrugs. Now she's thinking foie gras. "I guess into town." As they cross the bridge, Emma hums Springsteen's "Empty Sky." "I woke up this morning to an empty sky." She gazes at the skyline. Emma can't seem to get beyond this moment. It's as if she's reversing through time. Kangaroos, she read somewhere, can't go backwards. Be a kangaroo, she tells herself. This just makes her think of the Noah's Ark needlepoint that hung in her childhood bedroom with the caption, "Here come the animals two by two, the elephant and the kangaroo."

At night she dreams of kangaroos, smashing into walls.

Timmy got Tweedle Dee and Tweedle Dum. It was a minor obsession of her mother's. On the mantel in her parents' house, there's still a baby picture of them, wearing T-shirts that read "Seeing Double."

Emma hadn't really thought that much about her twin in years, but now she does all the time. But it's not as if she's having a flashback. It's more as if it just happened. As those towers came down, she felt her own self crumple. She wept when she read about bereft twins, searching for their missing half. About the forensic dentist who had tables lined with individual teeth like the tooth fairy.

In Chinatown her cell phone rings. Brian gives her a look that says, "Aren't you going to answer it?" and Emma shakes her head. Though she doesn't need to, she looks at the caller ID. It is her mother. Or maybe it's her father. Sometimes they trick her by switching phones. It really doesn't matter much which one. They've become almost interchangeable.

The conversation and concerns will be the same. Where are you? Why don't you call us? Sometimes her mother implies that Emma does this on purpose. Disappears; plays hard to get. But she doesn't. Emma doesn't give this much thought, her mother would be chagrined to know. It's what she does naturally.

After 9/11 her father gave them all cell phones—matching, only different colors. His was green, her mother's red, and Emma's was yellow. "We're a traffic light," Emma said when she saw them all together. He pays for the charges, but complains that Emma never keeps hers on, though she carries it in case she's buried in rubble. She plugs it in to charge from time to time, makes sure it works, tucks it in her bag and never looks at it again. Once Brian showed her that she had thirty-six unretrieved messages, but Emma didn't care.

She knows her worldview is askew. She thinks about giving people box cutters for Christmas. She herself wears razor blade earrings. She's been working on a piece of comedy called "Battered Homes and Gardens." She dwells on stories such as that Puerto Rican grandmother murdered by a person posing as a wheelchair trainer. She focuses on things like the people who fill gumball machines for a living or headlines that read "Virgin Found in the Trash."

There's a spot in a loading zone in front of the Union Square Café and Brian zips in. "This won't take long," Emma says. He gives her a nod. But it's a slow night at the Café and as she walks in, the tall, lean maitre d' eyes her. He gives her a knowing glance, then raises a finger as if he's about to say something, but she's out the door. "He recognized me," Emma says. She crosses the Union Square Café off her list.

"I think you want to get caught," Brian says. He loves her. She knows he does. That's why he goes along with her schemes. But Emma's not sure she loves him. That is, she loves him in his pieces, his parts. As her conspirator, her partner in crime. But Emma isn't certain she can love the whole of anything. Though she does love the thrills. And, though she's never admitted it, it's not the deed that excites her so much as the thought of getting caught. Interrogation turns her on. Being held against her will. In a cell of four gray walls. She likes to think about people tied up, torture, weird sex. Anything involving shackles is good.

It's a slow night in the city and they get too many offers to sit at the bar or "We can have a table for you in five minutes." They manage an antipasto at Gus' Place, but when she returns the plate, the host makes her pay. "Maybe we should stop returning the plate," she suggests.

Brian nods, but thinks it through. "But then that is stealing, isn't it? If we take the plate?"

"Oh, god," Emma rolls her eyes. "You are so literal."

They try to hit up Tribeca Grill for a beet and goat cheese salad, but no go. "Pickings are slim," Emma says to Brian who's sitting on the hood of the car, smoking a cigarette. He wants to go to Grand Hunan and order soup dumplings, but Emma wants to score. She keeps having to up the ante, heighten the stakes. "Don't you think you're just reliving some past trauma?" he says.

"Bad things happened to me," Emma replies.

"They didn't really happen to you," he tells her, flicking the cigarette away. "They happened to people around you."

"It's the same thing," Emma says, thinking that it basically is. There's a chill in the air. It's almost that time of the year when Timmy drowned. Their mother had a twenty-pound Butterball ready for the oven. The night he died, Emma was drunk. They all were. "Let's go to the quarry," Timmy said, but no one wanted to go.

The last thing Emma saw was his torn parka with feathers sticking out. *He looks like a chicken*, she thought as her brother disappeared into the woods. In the night she'd woken. In a dream she saw him in a dark circle, waiting, she thought, to be born. Later she realized he was just afraid.

When they get back to Brooklyn, they're still hungry. Emma puts her hand on her stomach as if she's pregnant. "It's growling again."

Brian drops her off. "I'll get a pizza," he says. "Pepperoni, okay?"

Emma nods. "Don't be long."

She's checking messages to see if her temp agency has called when Brian comes back with a pizza and a six-pack of beer. "Real food," he says, "labored for, paid for. Only the best for my girl."

But Emma's disappointed. "It's more fun the other way."

"It's your fix, isn't it?" He puts pepperoni and mushroom slices on paper plates, pops a few beers.

"I like adventure."

"Well, how about floating down the Amazon or sky diving in the Rockies?" Brian isn't someone who needs excitement. He's had enough to last a lifetime. His mother has that disorder of collecting things—

newspapers, toilet lids, old shoes. You can't even walk into her apartment. She never throws anything out. "Be happy with what you have."

"And what's that?"

"Well," Brian says, slam dunking a can into the trash, "you could start with me." He reaches over, kisses her. He tastes of tomato sauce and pepperoni. Brian pretends to drag her, caveman style, to bed. With his tongue he starts with her feet and works his way up, then works his way down. There are good things about being with someone who has a learning disability, Emma thinks as she comes.

In the morning when her temp agency doesn't call, Emma lugs her wash down to the basement. In the enclosed, steamy laundry room she finds a few magazines—*Tango*, for swinging singles, and a magazine about tattoos. She's reading about the Irish goddess tattoo when Jesus walks in. He gives her a big smile, his white teeth shining as if he's had them capped.

"Nice and warm in here," he says. Since he's not carrying a laundry bag, she assumes he's come for a place to smoke and play hooky. Instead he sits and stares at her. "So how's it going?" Jesus asks. He lives on the fifth floor with his grandmother. There's a mother somewhere down South and a father maybe in the Army. She feels badly for him, but it unnerves her—the way he stares.

"It's going. How's school?" He shrugs. She's pretty sure he hasn't been going to school for a while. She's pretty sure he hasn't been doing much besides hanging out. "What's your favorite subject?" she asks, not knowing what else to say.

"History," he tells her.

This wasn't the answer she'd expected. "I liked history too," Emma replies—until it caught up with me, she wants to say. "In fact I majored in it."

"Battle of Poltava, 27 June, 1709. Waterloo, 18 June, 1815. I remember things like that," he tells her. "Gallipoli, 19 December..." As Jesus recites a string of losing battles, Emma thinks that he must be about the same age Timmy was the last time she saw him. It's how she pictures her brother except Timmy was pale and Jesus is dark. Forever seventeen. An eternal child.

Sometimes she has what she calls "Timmy Sightings." He's getting on the subway, walking a hound dog in Prospect Park. She'll give a wave and then he's gone. When she read about amputees and phantom limbs, she got it right away. I've got a phantom brother, she said.

She remembers little things. The way Timmy kept shiny pebbles in a matchbox, the way he carved his initials into trees everywhere he went. When they slept in the same bed, they slept head to toe. At night she could smell his feet. He did her math homework whenever she couldn't. He shared everything with her. He separated the food out on his plate. Whenever she liked something he saved it for her. Every last morsel. What she didn't like, he'd eat that too. He cleaned her plate. If she stayed out late, he was her alibi without being asked.

They had the same reddish hair. The same squared features. Are you identical? dumb people asked. Still, it was like looking into a mirror and seeing yourself. They played a game. They would stare at one another and imitate the other's movements. She'd pretend to run a comb through her hair and so would he. He'd pretend to pick his nose and she'd mimic him. It was an odd game, but it amused them for hours.

Emma was fascinated with cases of mistaken identity, separated at birth. Those creepy gynecologist twins in Illinois who switched places on their patients and even their girlfriends and later their wives. And those two blond girls in a car crash. One lived and the other died and even their own parents weren't sure who was who.

What if I'm Timmy? Emma wondered when he died.

Of course she couldn't be. He was a boy and she was a girl. That was definite proof. But sometimes she envisions herself with breasts and a beard. Once in grade school she did a self-portrait with a penis dangling between her legs, and the teacher said she was sick. She had a friend with a strange birthmark; he said his twin had died in the womb and was reabsorbed into his skin. Emma waited for a mark to appear on her arm, but it never did.

It will be ten years this Thanksgiving. Each year her mother pulls herself together to put a turkey on the table. She always asks Emma to invite a friend. Three is an unbearable number. There must be four or six at the table. Never three. An even number, never odd. "Siege of

Stalingrad, July 1942; Bay of Pigs, 1961...." Jesus is still rattling off his history of battles when her clothes come out of the dryer.

As she is folding, he watches her. When she has trouble folding her white cotton blanket, he takes it from her. For an instant Emma thinks he's going to wrap her up in it and cart her away—though for what purpose she cannot say. Instead he presses it to his face. "This is the softest blanket I've ever touched." Then he closes his eyes like a baby falling asleep.

"You keep it," she says.

"No, I can't..." he tries to hand it back, but she thrusts it into his arms.

"Really, I want you to have it." When she gets upstairs with her clothes, warm and neatly folded, it comes over her again. The hunger she can't explain. She wants to be fed, like an addict, not food she pays for, but what's given to her. What she can take away.

When Brian gets home, she convinces him. "Let's go back to Union Square."

"You just got thrown out of there."

"I'm sure they don't have the same host every night." It's not like her to make that common criminal mistake—returning to the scene. She's never done it before. It's not like her really—to go to the same place twice, to return to the scene. Like the quarry. She couldn't stand how it was just a big hole in the ground. The hole, they used to call it. The long gray sides of the quarry rising. If you were alone, you had to tie a rope to a tree. That was the only way out. Timmy forgot that part. She never went there again.

"All right," Brian says, slapping his hand on the wheel. "Union Square." Anyway they didn't score last time. Like an ornithologist with a life list, she's got her restaurant list. She needs to take from the best. Driving across the Brooklyn Bridge, Emma gazes at the empty sky. Sixteen twins died in the Towers. Identical twins gazed into mirrors in search of the other. The widow of one stared longingly at the surviving twin until that brother's wife put a stop to it. Lately Emma's begun to think of herself as a special case; she was already a twinless twin.

Even fraternal twins couldn't bear having the other die in towers that were called Twins. She read accounts. There's no closer relation, experts say. Doctors report sonograms of twins kissing, battling,

26

clutching one another in the womb. Her own left earlobe was flattened before she was born.

She decides to skip the Union Square Café. Brian's right. It's too risky and there's no reason to hit a place twice, so they pull up in front of Gramercy Tavern instead. She's going to try for the blue Hawaiian prawns. It's, what, another birthday. Something to celebrate. She goes in and the young hostess approaches. "Just one? At the bar?"

Emma is pleased to see that the restaurant is crowded and the hostess has a list, a rather long one. "How long is the wait?"

"Oh about half an hour."

"You know," Emma says, twirling a strand of her long red hair. "I realize this is a rather strange request, but you see, my brother's going to graduate from college. With honors. Actually he has a really bad learning disability, but he made it through school. It's pretty amazing, don't you think, and now he's got his BA. He'll get his diploma in just a couple weeks."

The hostess is looking at the line of customers forming behind Emma and glances nervously at the packed restaurant behind her. She holds up a finger to one of them, indicating "Just a minute."

"I mean, I know this is an odd request. But he loves your blue prawns. I promised him some for graduation, but we can't really wait...." As she's speaking, a man comes up behind the hostess, but she doesn't quite notice him. "He's going to veterinarian school. He plans to specialize in goats."

"Excuse me," the man says, "but I've seen you before."

Emma's seen him as well. He's that tall skinny guy who kicked her out of the Union Square Café the last time she tried. She forgot they are under the same ownership. Emma backs up as he comes at her. "You just stay away," he says, catching her by the scruff of the neck as if she were a kitten. He's stronger than he looks and, though it appears that he's being affectionate, he's actually hissing into her ear, "If I catch you one more time, I'm calling the police."

He gives her a push into the street where Brian waits on the sidewalk. "Don't come back here," the man says. "Brother, sister, whatever you are. I don't want to see your faces again...."

As Emma stumbles on the sidewalk, Brian leaps to his feet. He rushes at the host who shoves Brian against a car. Brian shoves him back. Then his left hand—she knows it is his left because it has "LEFT" tattooed on the knuckles—comes up and slams the guy in the jaw. Before Emma knows what's happening, Brian's tattooed knuckles are flying—LEFT, RIGHT, LEFT, RIGHT—in the air.

This reminds Emma of touch typing class until she hears the crunch of cartilage as the guy's fist rearranges Brian's nose. A geyser of blood bursts as Emma jumps up and tries to pull the man away, but not before he lands a kick in Brian's ribs. "I'm going to call the cops if you aren't out of here in one minute." He straightens his tie as he walks away. "And I never want to see your faces again."

Somebody hands Brian a gym towel that he holds against his nose. Moaning, he gets up and Emma takes him by the arm as the crowd disperses. Her cell phone starts ringing and she turns it off. Brian is silent as they get into the car and she drives. "I'll take care of you," she sobs. Brian, head tilted back, is trying to wiggle his nose. "I'll clean you up when we get home."

"I can take care of myself," he sputters.

"C'mon, Brian," she says. "It was just a game."

"It's a sick game," he says, blood dripping down his hands. "And I don't want to play anymore." In silence they drive across the bridge. Emma doesn't look at the sky or at Brian with the stained cloth pressed to his face. She stares straight ahead.

They approach their building where the gang of kids lingers out front near the trash. They have doo-rags on their heads and a boombox blasting gangsta. The boys make a vague attempt to hide their joints. Jesus stands with his back to the wall, smoke rising behind him as if he's a smoldering fire. He stares with his dark, sad eyes as Brian rubs the wounds of his own lost battle. "Hey, man, what happened?" Jesus asks. "What happened to you?"

Eleonore Leonne Bennett, *Floating Ghost*, 2010. Photograph.

ALICE AT WORK

Alyse Knorr

honey locust patch now ivy now char
looks like fern looks real—must be
the seventh graders again, one tore up the rules
scraps of paper lettering the Bible
camp halls but from the bottom
up distortion details

Jenny your eyes look like eyes
inside of other eyes the rings
rotate around your arms and one
leg this must be a raindance
only all that falls from the sky is
hello
  you say you want to be
a mountain postcard your hips
closer to the sun back arched
thunderstruck spill but the day
that we met you were moving
and the laws say this will not change

unless
during the lunchtime assembly
someone were to act upon your body
and turn you to wine or glass
or rain

ALICE IN LOVE

Alyse Knorr

my eyes knot together
a map from the kit of stars glued
onto the pocked ceiling above her bed
and Jenny spread on top of me,
limb against limb, her hot breath
tapping a liturgy into my marbled ear;
her winter boots gauzed in stiff snow
in the corner and it was her feet all along—
that steady footing through the silk hillocks
along rows of pines cascading daily, ever green
ever whistling ever medicated—ever gone
skinny dipping holding some drunk
guy's hand smelling bourbon on his lips—
it was a concrete gully in the roof, really,
views of the city on all sides red and yellow
and blinking, the water chlorinated cold, and
how safe I felt today in the valley with Jenny:
her raw, chapped hand pulling me along
the crunching, ice-slicked paths—it wouldn't
have mattered if she was only taking me
out to get the mail. snow dropping from the pines
in thick rushes. my tongue running the grooves
between your knuckles Jenny your thighs
under the stained glass

OF DOGS AND DREAMS

Anne-E. Wood

THE ROOM WHERE Mom lay was covered in lilies. Everyone she knew had sent them and their sweetness filled the house. The cards hung on a string by the window close to the bed. That had been my wife's idea, to give the place some color. Now the morning light came through the slats. Dad squinted, but nobody turned down the shades. We stood there, the three of us, in our pajamas. That's all we could do—stand around the bed in the silence.

But what broke my heart, Dad finally said, folding his arms across his chest, *was how her dreams stunk. They reeked like street dogs because dogs ran through her dreams. In the middle of the night, she whispered those dreams in my ear. Still asleep, she confessed it all: how they came to her wearing crowns. I suppose they were kings.*

My wife—she was my wife-to-be then—looked at me as though I might have answers.

Those dogs took her down on the stairs, in the hallway, in the basement, the whole house full of dogs, running through the bedrooms, around the living room, up to the attic, their teeth ripped through her dress. And the tongues of those dogs, she told me how they flapped and dripped for her sex. Of course, she let them. She opened her legs, her nipples displayed, she fed them, she did not run or kick or put up a fight. They sucked and humped and slipped into her, one by one. She fell asleep in that dream like a tired sailor washed up on the shore.

She almost left the room then, my wife, she almost did, but she didn't. She stayed with me and closed her eyes, trying not to listen.

How could I rest with the smell of those dreams? They bled into mine. Dogs with maggots dripping from their nostrils. Dogs that had lived in garbage cans, whose mouths had sucked the bones of raw chickens, dogs that had eaten feces, that had sniffed the asses of dead bitches. Summertime dogs with no homes, no water, blood of discarded meat rotting in their teeth....

My father never faced us, never turned to the bed with the sheet pulled over her body. We watched the bald spot on the back of his head as he spoke.

I'm sure you kids would love for me to tell you a love story. How it will go on and on, the house you will build. The children you will grow and tend to like gardens. Maybe you won't, he said.

He picked one lily from a vase on the table, examined its petals and let it drop to the floor.

Or maybe you will. Until the dogs tear through your dreams and destroy the home you built together.

He rubbed his hands, the way the old do to keep the blood flowing.

Life is long, Christopher, he whispered, though that had been my brother's name and years since I'd heard him say it. *Too long. There is no peace. Not even when you sleep, not even for a moment.*

YOU HAD ME

Chloe Caldwell

YOU HAD ME when I was a teenager, so you got my best body, depending on how you look at it, though I was less comfortable in it then, than I am now. I had small tits that I thought were big, small hips that I thought were big, and legs that I thought were fat but were not. You had me when I was dyeing my hair super blonde from the box and had clear skin. I was so afraid to have sex because of the pain factor, so I clenched and clenched and clenched and you were patient with me for months and months and months until finally you whispered, "Relax," and I listened to you.

And you had me close to this time because I started dating you while I was still messing around on High Street with the abovementioned. You had me when you lived on Main Street. You had me live there. You had me fill up a drawer. You pretty much made me. You had me when I was driving to community college at seven every morning. You had me when snorting narcotics was my afterschool program. You had me when I thought I wanted to be a substance abuse counselor, not even noticing the irony. You had me when I drank Budweiser and loved the Yeah Yeah Yeahs. You had me when I was addicted to pills but also to working out. You had me when I would take a bunch of Adderall and then go to Kickboxing classes, getting my heart rate high as the sky.

And you had me when I was pathetic but didn't know that. Meaning I didn't know that and you didn't know that. You had me when I was sad and skinny and wearing clothes too big for me. A men's white T-shirt, jeans that were falling off my waist, a coat with a wool hood even though it was spring. You had me at my thinnest. You had me when I was scratching my face off. You had me when I stopped eating food (one Hot Pocket a day) and only ingested pills though I didn't chew them then like I do now. I snorted them, only.

And you had me at my prime. My easiest, my happiest, when I was light and dark at the same time. You had me in Williamsburg, in Brooklyn, in the summer. You had me when I was young and I knew it. You had me as a joyous, pacing, unemployed blonde girl saying please,

please, *please* can I do some heroin with you. Please. You had me when I was vulnerable with excitement. You had me when I was at the point where I would do anything that I shouldn't. You had me when I needed to party more than I needed to sleep. You had me when I was fearless in my ignorance. You had me after I'd learned how to make myself come. You had me when I had the ability to fall in love with any boy who lived in Brooklyn and read books and looked at me. You had me when I was so enthralled with New York City that I was falling asleep with gum and markers in my bed. You had me before I knew I was a writer but I read you some journal entries once when you were high and you told me they were beautiful. You had me before you died.

And you had me when I was confused and cold and adjusting to my first winter in New York. I didn't really know where my life was going and you made me laugh. You were a man. A French one. You had me when I had put on winter weight and was somewhat depressed about that. You had me when I listened to Of Montreal a lot.

And you had me when I was finding writing. You had me when my best friend and I shared a bedroom that had an Aladdin poster in it. You had me when I hadn't had sex in almost one year. You had me when I was binge drinking with my friends. You had me when I didn't take my writing seriously and you took me aside at the bar and said, "You just have to take your writing more seriously." You had me when I did Pilates on my carpeted floor every morning to make my stomach flat. You had me when I was coming of age, I would tell you. "Stop blaming your hormones," you'd say. You had me when I was insatiable for orgasms. You had me when we were touching every part of our bodies together and I would whisper in your ear, "I want you," and you would sometimes smile at that and other times look serious and you would always respond, "You have me."

And you had me when I was trying, trying, trying more than I knew. Looking back I was really trying. You had me when I was trying to live on the west side of the United States of America, even though I didn't know what I was doing there and I hated it to an extent. You had me when I would go to swing dancing classes and eat Valiums and Banana Nut Cheerios and you had me when I was a full-fledged nanny. You had me when I fell into a depression, when the only places I liked to go were a coffee shop and the doctor's. You had me when I stopped answering the phone.

And you had me when I was heartbroken enough that I couldn't even see. When I was waitressing and crying all the time, so much so that my boss said, "Give me your hand. Give me your hand. Whatever it is, it will be okay." You had me when I was a crying waitress and you should have known that, I should have told you that. But you didn't and I didn't.

Christopher Woods, *Ferris Wheel*, 2010. Digital Photograph.

GREYSVILLE

Tanya Frank

MUM USED TO leave the door open when she went to the toilet, and each month I would spy the thick wedge of her Dr. White's sanitary pad, stained with red-brown period, as it sat exposed in the crotch of her big knickers. The knickers had holes in them, tiny perforations that were oddly enough meant to be there. The pad was hoisted into place with a belt-like contraption. My brother Sam made the mistake of screaming once when he saw the scene rather than just swallowing hard, which is what I did. This presented Mum with the idea of chasing us with the offending article. She called it her jam rag and laughed at our squeals of disgust, thrilled that she had found a novel way of punishing us.

I knew not to talk about this, in the same way that I knew to keep quiet about what my stepdad Bert did on those nights out "up the road," as he called them.

It was grey up the road and it was grey where we lived, different tones of it, but grey nonetheless. Mum didn't seem to mind it too much. She kept herself busy by popping to the neighbors' for cups of tea.

"Ooh ooh," she called through the letterbox. "It's only me. Put the kettle on."

Later she traipsed back home with Skinny Doreen from St. Alban's Tower or Doppy Linda from Devon Court, bringing with her a fine cloak of smog from the North Circular Road. It stunk and brought on asthma attacks. My brother Sam got them all the time, whereas Bert, my stepdad, only got them when he was nervous.

Once inside our flat, Mum and the neighbors gossiped and smoked Players Number Ten in the kitchen at the yellow Formica-topped table. The cats did their business under that table, scrabbling around in a litter tray.

"For Christ's sake, Shirl," Bert shouted one night when the cats' frantic scratching in the litter got too noisy to ignore. "Can't you put that bloody thing somewhere else? It's putting me off me supper."

"Oh, for crying out loud, Bert," Mum said. "Where else can they go with us living ten floors up in the air?"

Bert didn't answer her. He hardly spoke to her anymore. He ate his supper off a tray in front of the telly in the living room and he stayed there the whole evening, moving closer and closer to the set to play around with the aerial. He loved that aerial even more than Mum, so in the end we married him to it. My brother and I put a scrap of net curtain around the metal prongs and pronounced them man and wife.

"Here comes the bride, all dressed in white," I sang as I walked the aerial along the top of the set while Sam declared himself the vicar, even though we were Jewish, and said, "Do you take this aerial to be your lawful wedded wife?"

"Shirl, tell 'em," Bert shouted to Mum in the kitchen who tore herself away from Doppy Linda and appeared at the doorway out of a haze of smoke, hands on her bulging hips, formidable in her crimplene smock dress.

"I'm telling you," she said, before disappearing back into the smoky gloom.

Bert sighed and pushed away the rest of his sausage and mash supper. He got out his asthma pump. Nothing about him shined anymore apart from a perfectly round bald patch on the top of his head. He looked tired from going up the road. Up the road wasn't just to the top of the street, as we knew it, but miles and miles along the straight, wide motorways in a thundering juggernaut lorry. His father had done the same work and his father before him, and they were all called Bert. Big Bert, Middle Bert, and Little Bert. Bored with the wedding ceremony, I ambled across the living room and stood at the kitchen door. The ping-pong of chatter bounced between the two women. Doppy Linda was comfortably seated at the Formica-topped table, as the captive audience. Mum discreetly slipped an LP on the record player. A blast of opera, really loud opera, flew into the living room and made Bert grimace. It never bothered Mum that she was the only living soul on the council estate to like such music.

"Listen, you'll like it," she said as she waved her hands around the smoky kitchen to "The Love Duet" from *Madame Butterfly,* conducting an imaginary orchestra, her voice straining to reach the high notes.

Doppy Linda, who seemed to be enjoying herself until then, turned her nose up and looked at the clock and said, "Oh, is that the time already?"

Then she got up to leave in the midst of the first aria when the pitch was sufficiently piercing to shatter a glass if we'd had one, but as it was, they'd all been broken and we kept to Tupperware beakers, stained Tupperware beakers that smelled of spaghetti bolognese.

The music stopped. The two women emerged from the kitchen, their Friday evening gossip over.

"I'd better get the ole man's dinner on," Linda laughed, looking at her watch. "He'll have my guts for garters."

Bert nodded as if to suggest she had overstayed her welcome and then he followed her to the door with his eyes, looking her up and down. Linda slammed the front door hard and we heard her stilettos click-clacking along the corridor.

"That woman doesn't know her own strength," Bert said.

"I think I'll go for a little walk," Mum said, bending at the knees, warming up. We all knew what her little walks entailed. Aside from opera, Mum's other passion in life was rummaging; be it for furniture, clothes, ornaments or oddments. The estate bins were the perfect place to salvage such items and Mum frequented the site just enough to keep our house full of clutter.

"You don't need anything else," Bert said without opening his eyes.

Mum didn't answer him, she just looked at me, lifting her brows and widening her eyes. It was a request for me to accompany her. I felt obliged, even though rummaging was an embarrassing business for a girl on the cusp of puberty. My biggest fear was seeing Nick Woodward, or Woody as we called him. I was more smitten with him than ever those days and I knew that he frequented the rubbish bins. He bragged about setting fire to the cars in the area and using spray paint to write "Fuk off you Kunts" on the Caretaker's garage door. Mum said if he was going to do such things he should learn to spell properly.

"Woody gets the most detentions in the whole class," I boasted as we waited for the lift to arrive.

"Bloody lift," Mum said, giving it an impatient kick. Then she returned to bouncing the pram in anticipation of our little walk. The pram was acquired at a jumble sale. The cumbersome thing stood by the front door, making it quite an effort to get in or out of the flat. Mum used it for shopping, jumble sales, and rummaging.

"I've written his initials on all my school books," I said, as the lift arrived and a whiff of stale urine seeped out. Mum entered backwards, stepping over the puddle, pulling the pram in after her, and wedging the handle up against her bosom. I squeezed in on tiptoes, attempting to evade contamination. Taking a deep breath and holding my nose, I pressed the button for the car park.

"I think he likes me," I said, after jumping out of the lift and adding to the array of wet footprints on the slippery red linoleum. "At registration, he turned his eyelids inside out and stared at me."

"Umm," Mum said, trying to maneuver the pram back out of the lift.

"He chased me with a chicken foot that he got from the butcher. He could make its claws move by pulling on a tendon."

"Umm," Mum said again, and I could tell her heart wasn't really in it.

"Annie asked him out for me last Friday in P.E. He said I was too fat. If I do a hundred sit ups a day and don't eat any more of the mint creams...."

Mum had a far away look on her face. I held tight onto the side of the pram as we jostled down the concrete ramp and along the walkway. The bins loomed so close I could smell them. Mum was smiling; she hadn't been rummaging for a few days.

"If he's at the bins, can we pretend to be chucking the pram away?" I asked. After a pause, she answered me; perhaps it was due to the fact that my question had the word "bins" in it.

"Don't be such a snob," she said. "And will you stop blimming well going on about that boy? He's from a no-good family and you're too young to be fancying boys."

"But, Mum, I'm twelve and three quarters now. Dawn Johnson is only eleven and a half and she's got a boyfriend already."

"Well, Dawn Johnson isn't my daughter," Mum said. "And while we're at it, you're not fat, you're fine. Don't keep on about being fat. How many times do I have to tell you it's what's inside that counts?"

We made our way through the sprawling underground car park, weaving between dumped and burnt out cars. I winced at the sound of our intrusion—the squeaking pram, Mum's labored breathing and the crystal beads of shattered windscreens grinding beneath the pram wheels and our steps.

Mum let me wait just beyond the huge metal bins. I stood far enough away to disassociate myself from the task but close enough to watch her outline come to life then fade under the car park's blinking fluorescent light. She worked deftly at her craft, leaning so far into the huge metal bin that I thought she might topple head first into the vast container. Luckily, the broad blackened soles of her feet in her fat Dr. Scholl's kept her grounded. Each time she rose from the endeavour, she inspected her find, measuring it with keen, squinting eyes.

Mum lingered over the highlight of the loot, a posh frilly dress fit for a bridesmaid or a Catholic girl at her confirmation. It must have been earmarked for me as it was much too small for Mum, and besides, she held it aloft as opposed to up against her bloated belly. There was an array of boys' and men's trousers. Mum hauled them out and selected those she would keep with no less deliberation than choosing pick 'n' mix from Woolworth's. She stacked furniture and bric-a-brac in a pile beside her and draped clothing over one arm until it became too cumbersome, whereby it was placed atop the bric-a-brac, forming a bundle that soon became a pile and finally a mountain.

When Mum stretched her arms into the air and brushed the dirt off her hands, I knew we were close.

"Tamar, come and help me," she said, much too loud for my liking.

I darted out of the shadows and we piled up the goods onto the lumbering pram—an assortment of clothes, shoes, a sea green ashtray coated with soot, and a coffee table with a missing leg. Covering the load with a crocheted blanket, we began steering it back toward home.

"It just needs the leg glued back on," Mum said, revealing a stubby table leg sticking out from her pocket. Then gathering speed in her desire to return home and sort everything out, she misjudged a corner and ran over my toes.

"OUCH," I squealed, as the pram almost careened into the wall of the car park. And that's when I saw him approach—his unmistakable wiry frame, oil-stained jeans, and determined strut.

"Woody," I said, in a voice so low it was pitiful.

"Jumble Princess," he remarked, his face lighting up as if he was genuinely pleased to see me, as if my fears were totally unfounded.

I stopped dead in my tracks, and I felt Mum stop too, both of us dwarfed by the mound of rubbish in the pram. Mum reached out a grimy hand, redistributing the load, making a steadfast claim to her prized possessions.

"Good evening, Jumble Queen," Woody said to Mum, bowing like a thespian and clasping a family size box of Bryant & May matches close to his chest.

"Don't you 'jumble queen' me, my boy," Mum responded. "Facetious little blighter."

"Facetious? What, you gone and swallowed the dictionary?" Woody asked. He shook his box of matches like a skilled percussionist and was gone, eyes scanning the concrete horizon.

I loved Woody's eyes. They were intense, narrow, and so close to his nose that they set him apart from other boys. Bert said those eyes made him look shifty.

I tried to follow Woody through the shadows, to have one last look at his nimble body and long legs as he gained ground on us.

Mum sped up again, regaining control of the vehicle and planning the evening ahead.

"There's some nice bits in there for you, Tam; I think you'll like them." I knew I was in for a night of trying things on, things that other people didn't want. Cast-offs.

Bert was asleep by the time we arrived home, the aerial on his lap and the television flickering in bursts of static.

"Oh, that was just what I was after," Mum rejoiced, pulling item after item from the pram. "It only needs a good wash and a stitch. Look, I can put a zip in here and a button there, take it in here and out there." I stood close by, ready and waiting for instruction.

"Turn around," Mum demanded as she threw the frilly dress with puff sleeves over my head. "Now stand still," she said, pulling and prodding at me with her hard, stubby fingers. "Breathe in, breathe out, arms up, arms down."

I looked down at myself in the garment, at the way the fabric ruched in under my breasts and flared out from my waist. I lifted my arms, felt the dress rise above my knees, and that's when I saw the stains, faint yellow circles of perspiration.

"That's nothing that a bit of Shout won't fix," Mum said.

I clamped my arms back down to my sides, the evidence concealed.

"That's the find of the night," Mum said. "Almost regal."

"Like a jumble princess," I added, wishing Woody could get a glimpse of me in such finery.

"Umm," Mum said.

Finally, having exhausted us both, she reached for her sewing kit and sunk deep into the couch, gloating over her finds and the good fortune that a little walk could bring.

IN FLUORESCENCE

Christopher Phelps

One handled, dimpled body
folded over the other,

our toothpastes are kissing,
two tubes in a medicine cabinet

otherwise Rembrandt-unromantic,
its glass shelves lit like slides

in a microscope, its camel-color
painted metal cave colder under

closer inspection. *Inspection*,
one of those Latinate words

for looking: we see so many
specimens we hardly notice.

Too circumspect already, I know,
this scrubbed peony, baby still life.

May I plead innocence or
maternity? Anything in this

medicine is by now routine but
in love we say what's been said

in an echolalia, like a parrot
the Enlightenment thought

the paradigmatic stupid animal
saying without knowing why

what's been said's been said,
although nobody listens so

go ahead and say it, said Gide
with defensive and offensive

parry and thrust, one motion.
In bed at night I ask no one I know

to exist if I might endure pain
without disconnecting from it

the way that false Buddhist,
the cynic, does.

Brush your teeth and go to bed
where a warm man waits, I hear

the voiceless parrot
that is most of thought plead—

gone hoarse, I imagine
the parrot a Catholic cardinal

taught the apostolic creed, I read
in Buffon, grinning in his ink

an infectious grin. Smiling down
from a smile, in the night

of a difficult year, I reassess
in fluorescence my irises

colored earth or sky or water
and always, whether cold

or re-embered, a tiger's-eye fire
twice escapes my black holes.

Dilated or contracted, what lies
in wait is nothing but the daily

beatified: time grinds that we
might de-degrade, claims the body

tangling into sheets, the man
whose love is not bluster.

RED IS IN / WHITE IS OUT

Celia Bland

Inmates Must Stop Behind the Red yellow Line languorously Inmates
Must hum Show Pass At this Point No Mesh Sneakers at this glistening

Chapstick NOTICE No Underwire women Brassieres Red women
Shorts no women Short women no Skirts women sawdust No

Denim women Inmates NOTICE Cleavage Swag Bags in Library
No in daylight At This Point Highlighters red line Visitors pens This

torsos No Inmates May Sit in forbidden Reception at this point All
Containers Subject To objects Weapons Red corrections In searches

Library at this Facility has eaten one Walks on the move East Wing
angel Wing west No Green Pants women denim Contraband Cell

papaya In Population Phones facility subject Canteen in cells
TB wristwatch Red Pens Prohibited searches IDs Subject At This

stirring up the air NOTICE mesh Subjects Must be containers
Must be daylight red yellow lightbulb highlight at Searched Upon
        Entering

Swag Leaving Green No at this point Red Is In at no one
White Is Out

AN EXCERPT FROM THE NOVEL *HERS TO HOLD*

Heather Aimee O'Neill

THOUGH WINE ON Hudson was nearly empty and Elizabeth could see that her best friend Darah hadn't yet arrived, she scanned the room anyway so that no one would think she was there alone, then grabbed a seat at the bar.

Elizabeth had told her partner Nina the night before that she had to cancel going to Long Island because of a last minute deadline, an article on cooking with turnips for *Newsday*. She figured it was a harmless enough stretch (she did have a piece coming out next month) but now she was beginning to feel guilty. She was also suddenly hesitant to share the news of Nina's pregnancy with Darah—she wasn't sure how Darah would respond.

Darah liked to keep Elizabeth anxious. The summer Elizabeth's father married Ana, he surprised Elizabeth with sleep-away camp in the Berkshires. She'd always wanted to go and her parents had never been able to afford a week let alone the whole summer. Still, the only reason Elizabeth wavered was because she feared Darah would find someone to replace her. From camp, Elizabeth wrote Darah long letters on flowery stationery. In turn, Darah wrote her letters about taking the train into Manhattan, hanging out on Canal with a girl from their neighborhood, a sophomore named Molly. Elizabeth was convinced she'd lost Darah to Molly ("we started finishing each other's sentences!") and each time Elizabeth received a letter she'd spend that day with a knot in her stomach that no amount of horseback riding or swimming in the lake could unravel. But when Elizabeth returned to Brooklyn that August, tan and a full quarter inch taller, Darah never once mentioned Molly's name again.

She should have brought a book, Elizabeth thought now, or a magazine, maybe even her notebook to work on a piece she was actually writing—"Tips on a Caribbean Cocktail Party"—for a friend's book on entertaining. She ordered a Stella and took a sip. She hadn't eaten that night and the cold beer hit her stomach and bounced back before settling.

"Do you want a shot?" the bartender said, running his chubby fingers along the tip of his green Mohawk.

"No thanks," Elizabeth said.

"On the house."

Elizabeth thought. "Okay," she said. "Something bitter and sweet."

The bartender returned with two bright pink shots.

Elizabeth inspected the drink suspiciously. It was an obnoxious pink. They clanked glasses and took the shots, an explosion of acidity and syrup in Elizabeth's mouth.

"That's awful!" she said.

The bartender placed his hand over his heart.

"Look," she said, "you're trying too hard. It shouldn't be too bitter or too sweet. You need to be more subtle." She returned the glass. "And it shouldn't be this bright pink. It should be blush."

The bartender turned serious and Elizabeth realized she'd been unnecessarily harsh.

"I'm sorry," she said.

Through the window she saw Darah walk by, then back again, until finally she opened the door. She spotted Elizabeth and ran over. Her blonde hair was pulled back in a tight ballerina's bun. When they hugged, Elizabeth caught the nostalgic smell of white musk, the perfume Darah wore in high school. Darah had just come from a business dinner, and in her black suit she looked far away from the tomboy Elizabeth had grown up with in Brooklyn. She slid onto a stool and ordered a glass of wine, then leaned forward and placed her hand on Elizabeth's thigh. It took Elizabeth by surprise and she felt her muscles tighten. Darah laughed. "Relax," she said. "You're so tense."

This was just one of the reasons Nina couldn't stand Darah. It was not only that she touched Elizabeth, but that she touched everyone. She always had. She couldn't help it. When she spoke, she had to make constant contact with the person, even a stranger. Elizabeth tried to explain this once to Nina, but Nina just said, "Well, not everyone wants her to touch them. She should learn that."

"You look happy," Darah said when her wine arrived.

"Do I?"

"Are you?"

"I *am*," Elizabeth said. It was true enough, she supposed.

Darah took a sip and put her hand back onto Elizabeth's thigh. "Then why wouldn't you look it?" she said.

Earlier this evening, as Elizabeth dressed, she wondered which story she would tell Darah. That everything was going well? That everything was—what? What she wanted to talk about was the story that Darah already knew, that only Darah knew. The story of when Elizabeth was sixteen years old and came to visit Darah at college in Albany, borrowed Darah's license, and had an abortion at the local Planned Parenthood. Elizabeth's father thought she was visiting Darah to check out the school and Elizabeth had not told her boyfriend Peter that she was pregnant. It was her spring break and she spent nearly the entire week holed up in Darah's dorm room.

Elizabeth had been in love with Darah since they were ten years old, but it only became clear to her when Darah returned home from college with Luke. When Elizabeth visited the promenade, she could still remember that fall evening when she noticed Luke's hand on the back of Darah's neck and she felt that first jolt of desire—and jealousy. The realization that it wasn't jealousy of Darah—it was jealousy of Luke—his hand on the back of Darah's neck, the caps of her knees, and all of the other places Elizabeth had to endure hearing about when Darah would call home from school.

And so Elizabeth found herself a boyfriend. Peter was her piano teacher's son. They would hang out and smoke pot in his building's windowless basement in a half-finished room near the laundry. He had bright blue eyes and a cautious smile and he made her laugh. But that was all. As much as Elizabeth tried, she recoiled each time Peter touched her until finally she was able to detach her mind from her body. Then one day after school while they were making out, Peter looked down at her with his bright blue eyes and said, "Can you feel that?" and suddenly Elizabeth was back in her body and Peter was inside her. Three weeks later she missed her period.

The night before Elizabeth was to return to Brooklyn from Albany, she and Darah opened all of the cigarette packs Darah had collected

51

during her Semester at Sea. Darah and Luke had gotten into a fight earlier and after several phone conversations that Elizabeth drowned out with *Simpsons* reruns, they were no longer speaking.

"You should break up with him," Elizabeth told Darah.

"I don't know," Darah said. "He's the only person I ever want to be with—" she took a drag of a bitter Cleopatra King from Egypt "I mean, aside from you."

Elizabeth felt her heart, dull and heavy in her chest. She was exhausted from the week. Her body was still sore. She'd just had an abortion and was in love with her best friend and though the doctor at the clinic tried to explain the severity of her endometriosis, Elizabeth hadn't understood the implications until that afternoon when she borrowed Darah's student ID and snuck into the library to do research.

"What do you mean by that?" Elizabeth asked Darah.

"I don't mean like—"

Elizabeth shook her head and said, "No, I know. I know. I just—" she stopped talking so that she wouldn't cry. She had not cried once the whole week. She took the cigarette, careful not to touch Darah's hand, and turned away.

A moment passed and Darah reached back for the cigarette. She took a drag and exhaled slowly. "Do you want to be with me?" she said.

Elizabeth wanted Darah to love her. Maybe they would move to a beach town somewhere far away or live in the country in a blue trimmed house surrounded by pink azaleas—but Darah loved Luke. "I've thought about it," Elizabeth said.

Darah was silent. She flicked the cigarette stub out into the dark night. They were sitting on the window ledge and Dave Matthews played from somewhere down the hall. Darah turned to Elizabeth and moved in to kiss her, gently at first, then fully. Elizabeth could have kept going, but Darah pulled away. "That wasn't so bad," Darah said. Elizabeth sat paralyzed. She watched Darah hop down from the window and collapse onto the bed. Elizabeth wanted to talk about it more. No. She wanted to keep kissing. But Darah hid behind her economics book to review for an exam the following day. Elizabeth lit another cigarette and though her throat hurt she inhaled deeply and stared outside.

They had shared Darah's twin bed throughout the week, but that night Elizabeth decided to sleep on the futon across the room. She spent a good hour staring at the blue bubbling lava lamp and waiting for Darah to crawl under the blanket beside her. That never happened. It never would, Elizabeth was beginning to realize. Later there was a knock at the door, a very drunk Luke, and Elizabeth pretended to be asleep as Darah slipped out of the room. She did not return until the following morning.

Now, in the bar, Elizabeth wanted to hear Darah's version of the story. Did she remember that the cigarettes were Cleopatra Kings? Their bitter, almost coffee-like taste? Did she remember when Elizabeth came back from the library with a manila envelope packed with photocopied pages from a medical dictionary that told her she was likely infertile? "Well, we know that's not true," Darah had said later. But it was. Elizabeth's pregnancy had been a fluke. A stroke of— luck. A lottery ticket she tore up before realizing it held the winning numbers. Elizabeth never told another person. Not her father, nor Ana. Not Nina.

On the walk to the bus stop the morning that Elizabeth left Albany, Darah stopped and turned to look at her. "I'll have a baby for you," Darah said.

"What are you talking about?"

"When you're older and married and want one," Darah said. "I mean it." She smiled and Elizabeth wanted to crawl inside her and stay there forever. "You believe me, right?"

"Yes," Elizabeth said.

On the bus home, Elizabeth did cry. She cried because of the abortion, because she was so numb to her boyfriend's touch that she didn't realize she had lost her virginity. She cried at how much she wanted Darah but knew she could never have her. She cried for how long she had lived in this place without hope and how she would continue to do so. But more than all of this, she cried because the kiss had felt exactly right and because of what that meant for her life—a new life that she did not want.

But instead of telling—or retelling—that story tonight at the bar, Elizabeth fell into questions about Chicago, Darah's family, her job at the new law firm. The conversation filled up a good hour and several glasses of wine, but when Elizabeth got around to asking about Luke, Darah dismissed her with, "Luke's Luke." Darah had started to talk this way about her marriage shortly after the wedding and that's when Elizabeth truly knew she was over Darah—when she was no longer glad to hear that she and Luke were having relationship problems.

Elizabeth was about to reveal Nina's pregnancy when Darah took a sip of wine and said, "I'm thinking about having an affair."

Elizabeth paused before she responded. She suspected that this was probably Darah's way of sharing news about Luke. She noticed that their glasses were almost empty and she ordered another round. They watched in silence as the bartender poured one glass of wine and opened another bottle to finish pouring the second. "An affair?" Elizabeth said after he left.

Darah rolled her eyes as though it were already old news.

"Is there someone in particular?"

"Not really."

"Then why?"

"Why not?" Darah said. She thought. "You know, you're right. I do need to find someone."

"Is Luke—"

Darah laughed. "What do you think? Do you think he's having an affair?"

"How would I know?"

"Nina hasn't said anything?"

Though Luke and Nina were cousins, aside from having mothers who happened to be sisters they had absolutely nothing in common and barely said hello to each other at their family's Christmas party. "No," Elizabeth answered.

Darah ran her finger along the rim of her glass. "Have you ever had an affair?"

"Have I ever cheated on Nina?"

"Don't put it that way," Darah said.

Cheated. The word hung in the air between them.

"I've never cheated on Nina," Elizabeth said. "I would never."

"I remember when I felt that way," Darah said.

Elizabeth had wondered whether Darah considered their kiss in college cheating on Luke. She wanted her to think it was cheating, to feel guilty about it. She wanted it to have meant something to Darah.

"I've been with Luke for thirteen years this fall," Darah continued. She propped her elbow on the bar and rested her chin on her open palm. "This summer was our third wedding anniversary."

"I know," Elizabeth said.

Darah straightened. "I'm drunk," she said and met Elizabeth's eyes.

"You are drunk," Elizabeth said.

The bar filled with a Saturday night crowd, drowning out Nick Drake's voice.

"Can I sleep at your place tonight?" Darah asked. She looked up at Elizabeth. It was a long, drunken stare. "I don't want to be alone in a hotel room."

Elizabeth felt heat rush to her face. "I'm not the *someone*," she said.

"Get over yourself!" Darah said and laughed. She picked up Elizabeth's hand and examined her palm as though she was trying to read the lines. "I do think he's having an affair," she said.

"I'm sorry."

"I'm drunk," Darah said again.

"Let's go."

Outside the sky was starless with clouds. The cold air burned Elizabeth's lungs. The snow came down in big flakes that melted as soon as they hit the pavement. Darah leaned her head on Elizabeth's shoulder and hooked her thumb into one of Elizabeth's belt holes. The embrace felt secure and comforting and for the first time that evening, Elizabeth allowed herself to soften to Darah's touch, the smell of alcohol and musk.

When they got into the apartment, Elizabeth deposited Darah on the couch and went to make peppermint tea. It was nice to be back home, to focus on something as simple and domestic as boiling water. Elizabeth finished making the tea and kneeled down on the floor next to the couch.

Darah lifted herself up and reached for her cup. She took a sip then sat up again and put her cup onto the teak side table.

Elizabeth handed her a coaster.

"Since when do you care about that kind of thing?" Darah asked but took the coaster anyway and placed it under the teacup.

Elizabeth didn't care, but the side table was from Nina's parents' basement and other than the large leather ottoman they'd brought from Nina's old studio, it was the one thing in the apartment that they took care of.

"Who do you think he's sleeping with?" Elizabeth asked.

Darah took another sip. "Tea is always better when someone else makes it for you," she said. She kissed Elizabeth on the cheek. "Thank you," she said, her lips lingering.

Elizabeth closed her eyes—if she turned her face an inch her lips would meet Darah's—then opened them and pulled away. Darah studied Elizabeth's face and tucked a piece of hair behind Elizabeth's ear. Elizabeth knew she should tell her to stop, to stop touching her and looking at her, but that wasn't what she wanted and so she didn't. Darah turned to stare at the wall of books behind the couch. She held up her hand and examined her wedding band, a sliver of gold. "Are you in love with Nina?" she asked.

"Yes," Elizabeth said. "I am."

"Minutes ago you wanted to sleep with me."

Elizabeth opened her mouth but nothing came out. "That doesn't mean I would have," she finally said. She needed to clarify: "That doesn't mean I don't love Nina."

Darah sat up. "I should go," she said.

Elizabeth felt like she was being tested. "I'll call you a car," she said.

"I'll get a cab." Darah stood. She reached for her jacket and looked at Elizabeth. They walked to the door. For a moment, it seemed like Darah was going to lean in for a kiss, then she pulled away and said, "I do love Luke."

"I know you do." Elizabeth took a step back. "Nina's pregnant," she said. She realized then that she wanted the announcement to hurt Darah.

"I see," Darah said. She buttoned up her jacket—slowly, Elizabeth noticed, as though she wanted to be stopped—but then opened the door and walked out.

Elizabeth sat at the table with her cold tea. She should have gone with Nina. That's where she belonged. She stared out the window at the snow. It was coming down hard and sticking to the ground. She knew Darah would never find a cab on a night like this, especially a Saturday night. She imagined her waiting on the corner until she finally resigned herself to the subway. She saw her walking into the pristine hotel room, fingers and toes burning as they adjusted to the warmth, then putting on the TV and falling asleep across the bedspread, alone and lonely, just as Elizabeth now felt in her own home.

WHAT FORCE I KNOW

Elizabeth Tashiro

March 11, 2011, Sendai, Japan

I.
When Goji berries became popular in the U.S.,
my mother sang their benefits.
She thinks it only fitting that a berry
with the same name as my grandfather
should be so healthy.
My father is humbled
by her good thoughts of his father,
who he still talks to when he drives home late at night, alone in his car.
She also says it's only right
that the berries are a little tart.
When I was younger and he older, we played Chinese Checkers.
His fat, soft fingers with thin hairs between knuckles
would shake as he moved a marble from one hole to another,
and then he'd hit another marble
and send the whole board rolling out of place.
He'd say something of a half-swear, like "Damnit"
or half-Japanese, like "Oh-sha."
Hearing the commotion,
my grandmother would rush into the room
to scold Goji for getting so upset
and to help us put the marbles back in their places.

II.
The Japanese Ambassador's tie is crooked.
A tired, dark blue that looks a little smokey,
it slants the same way his eyebrows and eyes
slope up toward each other, as though in question.

Bags under his eyes melt down into his cheeks,
and I see light brown age spots.

III.
I can see a faded house on stilts in Niigata, overlooking their rice fields.
Potted plants full of white petals on their porch,
like my grandmother's garden in her backyard in Chicago.
My cousins wear fragile silk that dries on lines.
I had to ask my father where our family is.

IV.
See the stillness of white plastic sheets neatly draped over rows of crops.
I think of the pains that a farmer took to lay that seed,
slowly holding each one in his palms,
walking the length of his farm with heavy feet seeping into soil.
The farmer is parent to his ground and mends the earth to keep
     looking upward.

V.
Unable to cool down, I think of Chicago summers
and playing in my grandparents' yard.
A limb of the tree in front of their house is almost within reach.
I'm nine, and I've never climbed a tree.
There are no trees to climb in Torrance.
Uncle Johnny would hoist me up to sit on that branch.
I never climbed farther—that was enough.

VI.
Sometimes I am one of my father's sisters,
and I remember the four ginkgo saplings
that Ma brought back from her trip to Japan.
Only one of them lasted.
It grew the height of our heavy brick house in Ravenswood.

I always imagined the leaves were fans, like palm fronds,
and cooled myself with their thin wax hearts.
One day, in the years when she was just beginning to show ache in
    her steps,
she asked the youngest, Johnny,
to rake up the leaves and dead tomato plants
and any other mess overgrown with age.
Hours later, we found him hacking away at the ginkgo.
Some of us yelled. He couldn't tell
it was living. Ma didn't say anything.
She slowly moved off the back porch
and went back to washing rice in the sink.

THE HOLE

Michael Sharick

THE HOLE MEASURED twelve feet across on the long side and ten feet five inches deep. The walls sloped hard, just a few degrees shy of vertical. Rock fragments revealed the strata of years of tilling and plowing, a naked cutaway into the underground. Bits of rock stuck out from the sides, amputated by the bucket loader, bleeding sap and water—good solid footholds if only the boy was strong enough to pull himself up. Crispy orange leaves twirled and danced above, some of them falling to the soft powder bed of earth and twigs and husk at the bottom of the hole.

Billy descended the hill carrying a new .22 caliber rifle, a black Hefty Cinch Sack slung over his shoulder. The sack bounced against his back as he walked. There was a forty percent chance of rain that day, and he wore green rubber shit-kickers, camouflage fatigues, and a camo-patterned Carhartt jacket, a pink numbered tag fastened to the back with an oversized safety pin. He also wore blue latex gloves that fit tight over his massive, calloused hands.

At midmorning Mary was still in her white silk nightgown. It was getting late and Billy would be home soon, but she was persuaded and she shoved a green stuffed dinosaur off the bed and spread her legs a second time.

At the bottom of the hole the hulking stinking mass lay, the stump where its head used to be leaking blood and mucus into the earth. The carcass was white, just a small patch of black on the neck below where Josh the Vet had made his initial incision. The boy had asked why do they have spots and Josh the Vet said because if they had stripes they'd be zebras and this was not at all a satisfactory answer for the boy.

    The engorged udder sagged between the stiff hind legs, the hooves still matted with alfalfa and manure. One of the teats had hemorrhaged and burst, and milk stained the bed of leaves and soil. Josh the Vet said this might happen, when he told Billy that absolutely under no circumstances could he milk her just one more time. The sour mess collected in a pool and mixed with blood and dirt and the boy poked and stirred it with a stick.

Billy laid the black Hefty Cinch Sack in the bed of the white 2005 Chevy Silverado pick-up. He was expecting to call Josh the Vet and tell him that he had found the fox and yes, it was behaving erratically, and yes, it was coming too close to him, and yes, it actually was really honestly foaming at the mouth. And yes, he put a clean shot through the torso. Josh had explained how a shotgun wouldn't do, how the animal's head would likely be destroyed, and it would be impossible to test the brain. He would have to use a small-caliber single-shot rifle at close range to compensate for the firearm's limited accuracy. And if he managed to actually find and kill the fox—Josh had identified the bite marks—he would have to be careful not to touch it as he collected it. Billy asked why they had to keep doing all this testing. Four head had been lost and buried already and they'd all tested positive, and why couldn't they just kill the diseased animal. Josh the Vet told him they needed to test every animal—it was for science. Billy was a dairy farmer, his father was a dairy farmer, his grandfather had been a dairy farmer; Billy thought science was something that happened to other people.

But he bought a brand new gun off his cousin Mel, who was the mailman, and a box of Hefty Cinch Sacks from BJ's and a three-pack of blue latex gloves from Wal-Mart, and every day after the four a.m. milking he hiked up the hill looking for the fox before he had to be back at ten to prep the noon milking, and then this morning he found it and killed it and stuffed it into the Sack and was home before nine, and he laid it in the bed of Josh the Vet's white 2005 Chevy Silverado pick-up, which was already parked next to the bucket loader in front of the house.

Mary pushed herself farther down so she would stop hitting her head against the wall. Josh the Vet was excellent, she thought, because he was a doctor and understood about bodies and organs and flesh. He called her by her first name and brought her gifts from Albany where they have nice shops, and he was gentle and firm in conversation and in bed.

She had watched him when he told Billy they'd have to put down another, and he was sorry, he really was, but there could be no chances taken with rabies. She had watched her lover, the veterinarian—who'd gone away to school and come back home—she watched him talk to her husband, his friend. Josh had touched Billy's shoulder and told him it was a good thing that he'd found such a good deal on that bucket loader last year, it was in great shape, and how it'd cost so much more to rent a backhoe every time, and how maybe Billy could sell it if he really needed the money. She didn't watch them put down the cow.

Josh was so tender with her, and she knew it was getting really very late, but he whispered in her ear and she had an orgasm without even trying, and he said her name again and stiffened inside her, and she heard her name a third time, but it was deep and muffled, and they both heard the front door slam and the heavy footsteps in the kitchen downstairs.

The door to the mudroom was open again, and Billy kicked it shut. He called for his wife that Josh was here and where was the boy his boots and slicker were missing. The kitchen smelled of burnt coffee and laundry. A yellow strip of flypaper still hung from the ceiling. The faucet dripped, leaking well water into the sink, plinking forty-two drops a minute into the stained basin. It had been leaking since August and Billy had been meaning to fix it, and the broken screen on the sun porch, and the creaky bathroom door. He had a vague notion that he could tackle all of these right now before the noon milking, and that he might even squeeze in a shower first, and he climbed the stairs to the bedroom, still wearing the blue latex gloves, still calling his wife, still carrying the brand new .22 rifle, and he turned the knob of the bedroom door, and this one creaked too Goddamn it, and he kicked it and it flung open and knocked against his dresser, and he saw his bed, the full-size that was not quite big enough but was all he could afford to buy from Ronnie at the furniture store, that the bed was made, and it occurred to him that his wife and son were tending to their morning chores, Josh to the animals in the barn, and here he was wasting time in the house when there was work, always work to be done.

There is always work to be done on a dairy farm. Cows do not take vacations, and neither do dairy farmers. The task should have been finished right away but this was the boy's favorite, the all white with one small patch of black just below the neck. The boy's pet that he'd named after his mother. The boy who had once tried to ride his dog like a horse and cried when the dog was hurt. The boy who was left alone in the running pick-up, his mother in the feed store, and he kept pushing in the cigarette lighter and then pulled it out and burned his little fingers and dropped it and almost set the truck on fire, but his mother forgave him. The boy who at his sixth birthday party made a parachute from a bed sheet and jumped from his bedroom window and broke his ankle and had to do his chores anyway. The boy who climbed down into the hole to say goodbye to his friend—a silent behemoth of a friend—but then could not climb back out again and he cried and cried louder at the sound, the din of the diesel engine, his father in the bucket loader gathering dirt to fill the hole. The boy could not cry loud enough.

Mary, her lover in her arms, on top of her, shaking, sweating cold silence and shame, her eyes wide, listened as her husband's heavy boots had plodded back down the stairs, listened as the front door opened and slammed again, listened as the bucket loader thundered with life, the hydraulics lifting the bucket, the purr of the diesel engine as the huge machine settled into gear. She listened from across the hall in her son's little room, in her son's little bed. She breathed.

TO SARAH AT PROVINCETOWN

Ann Lauinger

for SRN

Writing poems on shells, you said,
to give as presents. That's strange,
I thought. The sea's voice
is its own, those lives long gone
to the guts of terns and gulls,
the diners themselves someone's dinner.

It's your blood that speaks in the shell,
and your pulse the impulse
to concentrate ocean's billions
in one short spell. Well,
it's as healthy as salt-stinging air
to be refuted, and more bracing still

at your own desk. Clams, mussels,
and whelks wait on a towel,
naked and dry. Pick from your bouquet
of fine-tipped pens the color
for each metamorphic charm.
In the lamplight, emptiness shines.

Let every calcified page stake
your claim to occulted kinship,
Delphic quake and cry.
I guess you mean to repossess
each diatom, each soft
blind thing. But Sarah—why?

THE VIOLET HOUR

Ann Lauinger

Your cat is no connoisseur of sunsets
so you are alone,
the house dark and expectant
as prayer, when you swivel west.
The wide water's conflagration,
the convulsion in the sky
strike like judgment on the covered sin.

The noble ruin of another day.
You shrug old comforts around your shoulders,
havened. The spectacle—
violent sublime
stripped of cause or consequence—
tempts you to crouch at the lip of the abyss,
to peer at the foul obverse

of all you love. Fingering the hem
of Tragedy's pall,
you inhabit your habits like a mole.
What is it you would be forgiven?
From the radio a disembodied
"Deh vieni, non tardar" sounds sweetly,
as if the loving heart were all.

[UNTITLED]
Charity Stebbins

Everyone in the camp knows the healer can only cure their backs, their skin, their ailing rashes. She does this alone, with a clear glass of water collecting their rubble. But everyone in the camp goes over to her anyway, with swollen tongues from too much sighing, with modern hearts all cyber-white, their blue-edges, their murder ballads, their falling asleep when it is still light. They come with machines for deflecting their memories, cameras for images of the natural world. They stride in like ghosts on a horse. They pass a shower beside a wire coop and faces children make to frighten one another. They see her enter from a darkened karaoke room.

If you are not poor, why all these spells? I made a bad wish in the well, one that I am already regretting. One by one, they sit in a place in the wall.

THE TRAIN JUMPER

Maria Hummel

A FEW NIGHTS after we move to Hollywood, my husband takes me to a special screening of *Dr. Zhivago*, one of those masterpieces I have vague notions about and forever unfulfilled intentions of seeing.

We stand in line outside El Capitan Theatre with the grave faces of provincials who are trying to look worldly, get our tickets, and process inside. Under this ornate wooden ceiling, Clark Gable once performed on stage and *Citizen Kane* played for the first time. The air inside smells faintly like a very dry wine. Shadows feather the walls. Voices murmur around us, and I strain to hear someone famous. *Dr. Zhivago* also premiered here, and after the show we'll hear a discussion with the filmmakers.

Meanwhile the theater is filling, filling fast, and my husband and I scramble to find somewhere to sit… here… no, those are reserved… taken… here, in some plain seats in a left-side row far away from the screen. My best jeans and my curled blond hair settle into the chair with me, and I know them for the first time as clumsy appropriations of a glamour that is bestowed rather than bought, ordained rather than heated and sprayed. I hide my nail-bitten fingers.

The lights darken. The movie plays. It is about love and poetry, red flowers, ice, and a country that destroyed itself for an idea. It leaves me breathless. Here I am, finally in Hollywood, full of the love and hurt of the world, full of Lara. The self-awareness that shamed me three hours before transforms into an enormous longing to make something of myself.

From ages twenty-eight to thirty-three, I will live in Los Angeles, exactly the span in which my mother gave birth to her four children, and, along with us, the purpose—though not the meaning—of her adult life. Like many of my generation, I will have a long, hard time distinguishing between my life's purpose and meaning. I will leave the city with nothing but a thousand sun-struck memories, and sometimes only one.

After the movie, a group of elderly men takes the stage, and they arrange themselves slowly on stools circling a mic.

One of them was an art director on the film. His face looks whittled from wood, his cheekbones so sharp you can see the marks of a blade.

He tells us that the magnificent red flowers outside Lara's mountain house are all made of wax. The wax melted in the hot Los Angeles sun and the filmmakers had to race to finish the scenes. The flowers' glistening color came from their artifice meeting real California light. It was not love that made them so beautiful but the imminence of their destruction.

And did we remember the scene when Zhivago and Lara travel west inside a boxcar, and a peasant woman tries to jump the train? The film stutters as she hurls herself up, and then is caught by someone's hands and pulled into the car.

The stutter comes from the edit. The scene had to be shot twice. The first time no one caught the actress and she fell. The train wheels crushed her legs.

It was a sign of everyone's devotion to the movie, says the art director, that the woman made the leap again as soon as she was healed. That she refused to be replaced by another actress. This way, they could still use her expression from the first take, the one that shows she knows she will fall, hard, and she can't be saved from it.

EXTENSION

Cathy Park Hong

I need a wig to cover my sick head,
sold as real hair from a Dehli monger's
wife who said god willing why I sell it for
    that betel-stained-bastard.
Grown since virgin days, her hair's braided
    into my tired scalp, I used to have a ruckus of hair,
like a tree foaming with trumpet flowers
    shading my frayed nerves,
inherited from my kin who plowed out fields
into a thousand vine-glorious melons,
    til ghosts a-come collecting
in their petticoat cages, stubbing each fruit
    til they plucked him out
her womb and pitched her wet babe in the air,
and caped by a spume of her afterbirth,
he flew with the sparrows,
and he tasted the wind,
then he landed on a nest
    of bleeding branches.

HALLOWEEN

Alec Hershman

Birds crossing through the dinner-light
peel November's lid from a neighborhood—

the children are costumed, are calendrical
in the festival of wishes—they are learning

to inventory doors, to knock and to pass.

Their dreams contain tokens of October—
so too their pillows. Death is a joker,

crisp with ceremony, strobing in the pumpkins,
in the likenesses, little and deliberate.

The skeleton dips a hand in the bowl of a skull.
There is nothing we have not been afraid of,

lit with the dazzle of collection: witches and wayfarers,
pirates and aliens. They are learning how to scream

with the frenzy of accomplishment, the diaphanous wings
making a sound like leaves. They are shedding the curl,

the smattered sluice of amniosis, and their mothers
have healed like marvels—tiny blue distensions

where the cauls of blood had been.
And even before that, when mothers were Cleopatras,

the single clop of a broken heel
started something blue beneath a nylon,

a spray of wires blushing up the calf.

DESPERATE MEASURES

Kenneth Calhoun

FROM MY FULLY outfitted home office I heard the fury of dogs over the whine of my shredder. At first I ignored it. There are many dogs in the neighborhood and they often raised their voices in unison, apparently protesting some imperceptible offense. Then I remembered that we had let the elf out earlier to perform his secret nature rituals. I thought, Could the elf be the cause of this terrible ruckus?

Is the elf still outside? I asked no one in particular as I strode down the hallway. And because I did not address anyone specifically, I was ignored by all. I caught a glimpse of my eleven-year-old daughter's face down in her beanbag, unmoving. Teresa, my wife, continued to talk to her twin sister on the phone. As I passed her office, I could hear her say that she was crazy in love with me and that we were at each other like rabbits.

I bounded down the stairs and, from the foyer, could now discern that the barking was indeed coming from our back porch. I passed through the kitchen and threw open the back door. There were two dogs barking at something cornered under the raised deck of the patio. Seeing them put me in a minor rage. They were so focused on their victim—surely the elf—that they weren't aware that I was but a kick away. I aimed the first one at the closer of the two attackers, the smaller brown dog. My foot caught him on the top of his head. He jumped back in surprise, yelped, and retreated to a spot on the driveway, with his big white companion drawing back as well. They shouted obscenities at me and I returned them, stooping to pick up a handful of gravel and throwing the fistful at them like birdshot. It was my intention to blind them. At this, they tore down the driveway, cursing over their shoulders, but continuing down the drive.

Get! I shouted. I ran at them and they retreated. They disappeared into the woods, the small one loping like a bear and the other trotting like a proud pony.

With the dogs gone, I got down on my hands and knees and peered into the slated darkness that had gathered under the patio. It took a second for my eyes to adjust, allowing me to see the elf cowering in the far corner. Its little hands were covering its little face and its knees were shaking. Elf? I said. That you?

It said nothing.

Come on, elf. Come to me. The dogs are gone, I said softly. Its hands came down from its face. I could see the horror there and I used it. Come on, quickly, before they come back.

At that, it rushed to me.

I held it to my chest and brought it inside. Feeling its heart beating that way—the trembling little body—brought back my fury. To know how terrified it must have been. The elf had shit itself, and the little green tights were a mess.

Once safely inside, I called down my daughter, knowing my wife was on the phone. Knowing also that, if my wife were to see me now as rescuer, as avenger, she would want to make love and there was no time for that. My daughter came down the stairs, squinting. Take the elf, I said, handing her the terrified creature.

What happened? she asked, concerned. She brought the elf close to her. Then her nose picked up the shit smell and she held it away by its Peter Pan collar. I could see that her hand was shaking—something I had been noticing lately.

Didn't you hear the dogs? I asked.

What dogs?

The little brown one and the medium white one.

Those dogs again! my daughter said. We had seen this pair sniffing around our yard plenty of times lately.

You take the elf up to your mother and clean it up, I ordered. I'm going to see about killing those dogs.

When I said to my daughter, I'm going to see about killing those dogs, I honestly didn't have the heart to kill them. I was thinking I would land some solid kicks in their sides, to firmly plant the association of pain with my property. Kicking dogs was a lot like kicking old suitcases, I imagined, and I looked forward to the sensation.

Yes, I was angry, but not murderous. It really did something to me to see the elf so upset. I suppose the reaction stems from the fact that the elf is so human-looking, but very small. Also, of course, I was indebted to the elf for saving my marriage. But my anger soon rocketed toward blind rage when I jumped in my frosted mint green 2001 Volkswagen Passat to chase the dogs down and, in the process of hastily backing out of the carport, scraped up against the metal support post. I jumped out and saw that the right rear door was badly creased.

Son of a bitch! I yelled. The capacity to kill bloomed in my chest. I jumped back in the car and tore down the driveway.

I sustained this rage twice around the block but, after failing to spot the dogs, decided to go home and check on the elf and see if the dogs had doubled-back looking for their victim. I parked in the carport and studied the creases in the car. The whole door would have to be replaced. The support pole was still firmly in place but badly scraped. I would have to paint it at some point. I scanned the property for the dogs. They would pay for all this, or at least their owner would.

Inside, I was greeted by Teresa, who was wearing her bathrobe. Her hair was wild. I could see her nipples boring through the silk. She came at me, cornering me in the kitchen, her gaze drilling desire into my eyes. Whoa, baby, I said, where's Kylie?

Upstairs. In her room. She had opened her robe. She was rubbing her breasts against my chest and unbuckling my belt.

I'd like to check on the elf! I told her.

It's fine, resting, she said, then bit my earlobe and added, Rock me, mister guy. She must have seen my charge down the driveway. This is how it was now: any display of masculinity triggered the response. It was a side-effect of the elf's magic that, at first, had been a godsend, especially after my year of sexual exile.

These days, however, Teresa's insatiable appetite summoned a little flock of sad realities, which we now endured in the kitchen. The first was that a man my age simply can't work up the jam ten times a day for weeks on end. This was in stark contrast to our earliest days as a couple, when the sex was unceasing for a good six months. Now it seemed that I had used up my lifetime surplus of erections a week or so ago. This physiological fact ushered in another surprising revelation, which I shamelessly exploited now as I mechanically turned my wife around and bent her over the kitchen counter. She whipped her hair to one side, revealing her slender neck and wiry shoulders. Pants at my ankles, hands on her waist, I spanked her with my pelvic bone, causing her fantastic ass to ripple faintly.

Each collision of flesh was answered with a moan. I looked beyond her smooth, muscled back—a vision I conjured countless times when I was living without her—and studied the yard beyond the kitchen window for the dogs. She climaxed quickly, remarkably, considering I was in no condition to even penetrate her. No matter these days, I had recently learned. So long as I went through the motions, she was able to find her way to orgasm. This was a devastating discovery. At the moment, however, it offered a quick-and-easy way out of an otherwise time and word consuming situation. Good thing too, because just as Teresa's ecstatic convulsions subsided, I caught sight of the white, medium-sized dog through the trees that border our neighbor's yard. The fucking audacity of those animals!

That was awesome, baby! Teresa said as I pulled up my pants.

I can't believe they're back!

I pushed her aside and ran out the door, charging at the invaders. When I got within a stone's throw I scooped up a stone to throw. I whipped it in their direction, managing only to throw out my arm. Damn! I howled, clutching my shoulder. I rubbed at it as the dogs grinned and trotted down the street. They lifted their tails, showing me their wrinkly winkies. This was the final insult. I started after them, catching a glimpse of Teresa watching me from the upstairs window, masturbating with vigor.

Oh, good Jesus, was all I could say to that.

We lived in the demilitarized zone between a very wealthy neighborhood and a very poor one, which some referred to as a ghetto. Our house sat at the outer edge of a band of middle middle-class homes about two blocks wide. Thankfully the dogs seemed to know their place as well as I did, never straying into the estates to the north, nor the tin-roofed shacks to the south. These certainly were middle-class mutts, no doubt rescued by well-meaning and/or cost-conscious residents of this warren of cul-de-sacs. They lacked the pedigree and German-language skills of the big house hounds, as well as the shark-eyed viciousness and beartrap jaws that paced the chain link dog runs of the poor. They were but puckish mischief makers, but they had gone too far.

I followed them around the block, passing my house twice, before they changed course by abandoning the loop and taking a road to the right, looking over their shoulders to see if I was still with them. I followed two yard lengths behind. My goal now was to find out where they lived, then confront their owner. The dogs seemed to know this and tried to throw me off, or at least put obstacles in my way. We were in a neighborhood that I rarely ventured into—one that had no fences, just smaller homes amidst the dense pillars of pines.

The dogs would drift from one backyard to another while I followed on the street. Every now and then, they would pause behind the house long enough for me to come to the conclusion that they had finally arrived at home. I imagined them lapping at a mossy bowl of water behind the shelter of the house and collapsing in the shade, grinning at each other.

I went to the front door of the first house they had disappeared behind and rang the doorbell. No one answered. It was a Sunday morning and likely that the homeowners were at church; it was that kind of neighborhood, that kind of state. I stood back from the house, noting the address, when out of the corner of my eye I caught sight of the dogs trotting down the middle of the street. They were already three or four houses away.

Animals! I yelled, starting after them. They did the same trick again a few blocks later, this time disappearing behind a house on the street parallel to my own—the street behind my street. In fact, the house they had chosen to hide behind was the house behind my house. Surely these dogs couldn't live here, I thought. I would have seen them through the knotholes in the fence, and heard their yowling at the sirens. I assumed they were just trying to find a shortcut back into my yard, where they could resume their persecution of my elf. After minutes had passed without sight of them, I decided to ring the bell. If this wasn't their home, at least I could get permission to circle the house and flush them out on to the street.

I went to the door and rang. I was only vaguely aware that an older couple lived here. When the door opened, the elderly man behind it quickly retracted a neighborly smile and called his wife.

Sorry to bother you, I said, but—

He cut me off with a wave of his hand.

I noticed that he had extremely hairy ears.

The wife, a gaunt steak knife of a woman, came to the door wiping her hands.

Look, the man said, directing her eyes to my face by pointing with his chin.

Hello, I said.

But the woman only looked at me then back to her husband.

You're an indecent fellow, the man said.

Excuse me?

Your indecency amazes me.

My indecency?

You need help, you and that woman. By God, I can't tell you how many times I've been tempted to call the authorities—

But we don't because of the little girl, the wife threw in. That poor little girl.

I'm confused, I said.

I'll say, the old man said. Do you think no one can see you? Don't you have the decency to close the curtains?

Or at least not do it on the roof or in the middle of your yard at all hours, added the wife.

Or on the hood of your car—the frosted mint green one—in your carport, he threw in.

Or up against the fence like some kind of arrest gone terribly wrong, she said. And so it went:

Or in the flower garden with the perverse use of some gardening implements.

Or in the magnolia tree like a couple of twitterpated mockingbirds.

Or in the loblolly pine, for that matter, rutting like nesting squirrels.

Or on the woodpile, sawing away like lumberjacks.

Or during a barbecue, painting each other up with some kind of tangy sauce and eating at each other like wolves in early spring.

Or on the little swing set, using the unyielding force of gravity as a sex aid because, after all, what goes up must certainly come down and that's rhythm that you can't help but exploit, sicko.

Hold on there. We've never used the swing set, I said. It's not meant for adults in terms of the weight it can safely support.

They ignored me. What you're doing is unnatural, the old man said.

You know it is, said the woman. At least your body knows it is.

They looked at each other gravely.

What exactly do you mean? I wanted to know.

Well, said the man, suddenly gentle, working to choose his words carefully, we couldn't help but notice that you haven't been able to—

The woman reminded her husband of his language: Rise to the occasion is how you put it.

Horrified, I turned to leave.

There are medications for that, the old man called after me. Amazing drugs, you know. In fact, I'd be willing to let you try some of mine, just to see how it works.

I picked up the pace, power-walking down the quaint path to their door, not only in the interest of putting this warped carnival mirror behind me, but also because I saw my dogs emerge from behind a house two doors down. They turned the corner and appeared to be heading back to my house. I bolted after them thinking I would catch them on my property again and make the negative association stick. But as I rounded the corner, I saw them pass my driveway without pausing, without a turn of the head or even a sniff at the air. I stumbled up to my mailbox and threw my arms over it, needing the support after my half a block sprint. We could be at this all day, I thought, noting that the dogs had stopped at the top of the street, sitting, as if waiting for me to catch up.

When I finally got moving again, the dogs stood and turned the corner, their legs scissoring as they passed out of sight. I lost them for a good twenty minutes. Without them to guide me, I wandered aimlessly, looking for evidence of their passing but also thinking—no, stinging—about one thing the old couple had said. One word actually: Unnatural. Of course they were right. Everything going on in my house was unnatural, all of it conjured by my little mail-order elf. But was it really that apparent? And their supposed concern for my daughter—of course, I had given plenty of thought to what this was doing to her. Those shaking hands: it had occurred to me that it was some kind of side effect.

Sometimes I thought she knew what I had done. Sometimes, during meals for example, I would catch her staring at me as her mother nibbled at my ears or ran her tongue up and down my neck. She seemed to sense a spell was at work, but had yet to come out with an accusation. The elf, she was meant to believe, was merely a novelty possession, a kind of pet that we had all come to love. She had yet to connect Teresa's unceasing, chafing passion for me with the presence of the elf. It had occurred to me that, when she figured this out, the elf could be in danger. My daughter had knitting needles. If she was to accuse me, I would plead my case, stating that I did it for love, to have them back. I did it to restore our family. I did it to get rid of that asshole Jake, who Teresa had started dating only eight months after kicking me out. Jake wasn't the kind of guy you'd want around your pre-teen daughter. Whoever heard of a doctor named Jake? It's a construction worker's name. Certainly isn't a father's name. With that as my argument, I didn't see her being able to hold it against me for very long.

It struck me, as I walked along staring mindlessly into parked cars and listening to the wind move thickly through the pines, that I may never see the dogs again. I stopped and looked up and down the street, which was lined with ugly houses. At the end of the street, I saw a kid—a teenager, I guess—bouncing a basketball on his driveway. There was a hoop and backboard attached to the eaves over the garage. It seemed to me that the kid was practicing his free throws. I was surprised to see a kid doing this in real life. I thought they had all switched to purely virtual living, since they were so rarely seen on the streets. When they were, they were inevitably thumbing at their phones.

But here was a kid moving around in the open air, sweating into his hoodie. As I approached I could see that he knew I was there, but was pretending he hadn't noticed me. He was thin—another surprise—but too short to be serious about basketball. Maybe he was just practicing for one of those carnival games, hoping to win some girl a purple bear filled with sawdust. His shoes were enormous and orange.

Hey, I said, you see some dogs go by here?

He gave me a sideways glance and set his big feet for a shot, bouncing the ball slowly. Dogs? he said.

His arms came up. The ball rolled off his hands and sailed into the hoop. He moved quickly under the net and was there for the second bounce. Naw, he said, keeping the rhythm going with the ball.

No? A little brown one with his bigger white buddy?

He shook his head, studying me. A faint smile appeared, but he reined it in, pursing his lips and looking down at the bouncing ball. It rang like a bell against the cement.

Have we met before? I asked.

He shot, then shook his head. We didn't meet, but I saw you that time.

What time was that?

He collected the ball and held it to his hip, now grinning openly. If I had a camera that day, you'd be famous. We'd both be. Online, anyway.

Holy shit, I thought. Has the entire city been spying on Teresa and I?

I counted, he said.

Here it comes, I thought.

You stopped and opened the car door for her thirty-three times.

He shook his head. So damn hilarious.

He laughed. I waited through it with a terse smile.

Then, in what I assumed was an imitation of me, he said, Baby, please get in the car, would you? Please? Baby?

He laughed harder, the ball dropping, hitting his foot and rolling my way. I stepped on it to stop it. So he had witnessed the last time I was on this street. It must have been just a little over a year ago when Teresa stormed out on me, after she read my emails. I drove after her in my then creaseless Passat and, yes, I did alternately beg and order her into it, to no avail. Two days later I was out of the house.

You'd drive like five feet, stop, get out and run to the other side to hold the door open, he recounted, looking out at the street as if seeing it play out again. And she would just blow right by you. I was all like, goddamn, that dude's in the doghouse for serious.

Well, I said, kicking the ball his direction, thing is everything worked out. A real happily ever after, I added.

Ha! he let out, like a cough. No way.

It wasn't exactly as though he was astonished, but the doubt annoyed me.

How the fuck would you know? You're just a kid, I snapped.

I started down the street. Maybe it's time to grow up, asshole, I said over my shoulder.

Dude, chill.

I felt him watching me, looking at my back. That's the view of myself I most hate—the view of my back, walking away, wondering what sign has been posted there.

I decided to head home. Walking around the neighborhood was like passing through some kind of gauntlet of shame. It was as though I was going door-to-door, selling encyclopedias maybe, and no one believed what was printed inside them. So maybe the facts were a little off, but the meaning was still the meaning. I felt like shouting this. The meaning is still the meaning, people!

But I didn't. Mostly because I saw the dogs again. They were actually flopped out on the front porch of a small yellow house at the end of the street, tongues lolling, rib cages rising and falling as they watched me approach. So this is it? Their true home? I started up the walk tentatively. They were staring, but not necessarily in a threatening manner. Still, if this really was their turf, you would think they would have issues with trespassers, let alone a guy who had whipped fistfuls of gravel at them. I took a few steps and nothing. No growling, no flashing of fangs. A few more steps and they looked downright docile, smacking their lips, looking up at me through their brows. Maybe they had realized they were at fault, that their behavior was unacceptable, and they had decided to own up to it like men. Or some men, actually.

It didn't occur to me to kick them or stomp them at this point. It's one thing to chase after them in the heat of the moment. But seeing them simply lounging, taking responsibility for their actions like this, improved my impression of them. Who knows? Maybe they were behaving the way they did because of the elf. Maybe it put off a vibe that they couldn't resist. They smelled the magic and it got in their heads, just as it had done with Teresa, and they lost all control. And maybe it had gotten in me, too, turning me into a raging, dog-hunting lunatic. I thought of my daughter's shaking hands. There's that, too. All of us affected, or infected. Side effects they don't tell you about. Otherwise, no one would order an elf online.

Regardless of the understanding we had mutually arrived at, they still shouldn't be roaming the neighborhood. There were laws against it. Their owner needed to know they were loose. I stepped over them and raised my hand to knock on the door. But I drew it back before my knuckles made contact.

Did I really want to have another conversation with someone in the neighborhood? What would they have to say about me? I didn't need to be judged or critiqued or assumed to be some new species of loser.

The dogs were looking up at me, panting lightly. There was no judgment in their black eyes—the very eyes I had hoped to blind earlier that day. Actually, there seemed to be a kindness in those tarry depths, a primitive and raw empathy. Maybe not so much in the eyes, but in the arched brows.

I sat down on the porch stairs and studied their forgiving faces. The white one was closest so I reached out and gave the fuzzy cone of his snout a friendly squeeze. I was struck then with a vivid memory. Something I had long forgotten from the very earliest years of my life, when I first ventured outside and played with the other kids in the streets of my suburban neighborhood. There was a dog that belonged to a family in the neighboring cul-de-sac. It was a terrier that was often seen roaming the neighborhood. This dog had a unique feature—a thick piece of white string, about an inch long, that stuck out of its head like a wick, or maybe a fuse. The boy who owned the dog explained that it had once been hit by a car, its head cracked open and its brains exposed. The vet put the dog's head back together and wrapped it tight in a bandage. When the bandage came off, the family discovered the string. The doctor told them never to pull on it, since doing so would mean instant death for the dog. It was very much like a pull-string for a talking doll, sticking out between its ears. I remembered how I saw the dog once, wandering the street alone, sniffing at the trashcans on the curb. I called it over and, after petting it for a while, couldn't resist giving the string a quick tug. The dog's eyes rolled back and it immediately stood up on its hind legs. It hopped about ten yards that way, like a kangaroo, before dropping on all fours and running off.

Apparently, I had not pulled hard enough.

My daughter rushed down the stairs when I came through the door. Come look at the elf, she said. It doesn't look good.

It was true. She had cleaned it and put it in a pair of fresh tights. The elf was curled up on a pillow in her window seat, wrapped in its moss cape. Its skin had gone slightly green and its tiny eyes were sticky with thick tears. It had a prickly mantis leg that it used as a hairbrush, but I could see it hadn't combed its hair after the bath. It was in bad shape. The scare with the dogs had done it, probably. They were delicate things.

Shouldn't we take it outside? my daughter asked, her voice quivering with worry.

She was right. According to the literature, that was the only way they could be cured of their many ailments—with nature rituals and herbal remedies that they gathered in gardens and woods: mushrooms and molds scraped off rotting fruit and danced over in tiny clearings between the trees.

Through the walls, I could hear the shower running.

The elf sighed a tiny sigh.

We can't, I said, taking her hands in mine and stilling the trembling with a gentle squeeze. It's too dangerous with those dogs running loose.

At the time, I fully believed this was my last lie.

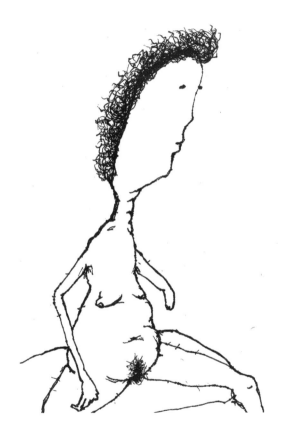

Kevin Strang, *amputee*, 2009. Pen on Paper.

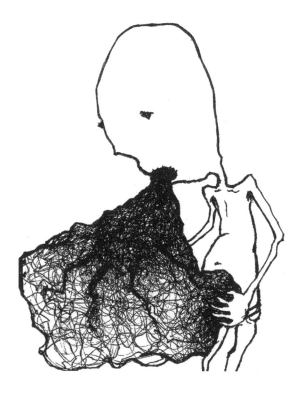

Kevin Strang, *sick*, 2009. Pen on Paper.

QUALIFIED NEGATIVE CORRELATION

Rick Moody

The following account, though unconfirmed, tells the story
    Of stars falling to earth, of Venus in view,
        Of mirage and its source
        (Reproductions are never perfect);

Be careful when walking in the dark,
    It is easy to see things that don't exist;
        Hazards include snakes, playful, intelligent,
    The inexplicable is complex.

Auroras, ribbonlike?
    War and suffering?
        Assume a leakage of buried things,
    Assume a small, well-ordered graveyard;
There were only two reasons for a young,
    Unattached woman to come to the frontier;

Before reaching the shimmering it disappears,
    The remote city on the roadway,
        Fata Morgana its special name.
    The woman's body was later found,
        But what of her boys?

Wonders and signs upon the land—
    I will always remember that somber march,
        The devil danced with glee across the valley,
    The country, just as God made it;

The Apaches, too, ceased to be—
  They lived in houses plastered with mud;
    Outrages were committed, others feared,

The wastes acted as a corridor, particles spiraling,
  Space by definition a void,
    The adventurers returned with their scalps,
And yet in return for plunder they were furnished with arms...

You crossed the river and now you are alone—

IMPERFECT

Ronda Broatch

Maybe the rope was cut, and the rain fell hard.
Maybe the year was wrong,
the bed wasn't prepared just yet.

Perhaps I will carry a little fire until I die.
A blaze to bring the cone to birth, bury the seed
the nuthatch might otherwise eat.

Deep in sleep your breath blesses my face.
We wait years and years.
Alders lace their hands across the road.

Maybe the rabbit has accepted the hawk.
Maybe the year was older than the child.
Maybe the pain had nowhere else to go.

So what if the river rises past our windows?
And why shouldn't fire have its day, its night,
the rain speak in steam?

If we put our feet close enough, the fire will lick
our soles clean. I've washed often in rivers.
In time this stone will wear away.

WHY I DECIDE TO STAY

Naomi Lore

The lot next door to me hustles
car repairs and weather forecasts.
Huddled around the oil-darkened
radio, the men stomp their feet in
the snow, and breathe clouds across
the naked, idling engines.
They have become my uncles,
like the uncles I had back home;
the ones that didn't look like
me or share my father's last name.
One of them sits in a green Jeep
every morning when I walk
north to the train—the windshield
fogs around his cup of coffee.
When he smiles at me, his face
broadens the way the sky
has leaned back on its elbows
to let these storms park across us.
On Saturdays, he helps me clean the snow
from my car without saying much.
The streets are less anonymous after a storm.
Even past Quincy and Gates,
there are husbands and brothers
I've never seen before, buried
in large leather coats,
leaning back on their shovels
beneath the white collarbones
of the laden trees.

Eleonore Leonne Bennett, *Alan with Lung Cancer*, 2011. Photograph.

BLUE ROSARY

Leslie Paolucci

These are not prayers. Hail Marys repeated

standing still and mute as pond grass,
blue-gray sentinel by the edge of the marsh

until the words don't even sound—

your beak reaps the plenty of the bog,
ends the peepers' song. You glide

like words—a hushed murmur

on prehistoric wings, you cast your ominous
shadow over the water. A soft whoosh, a flash

in cool chapels—the promise of something pure

of realization then crimson darkness. An enduring
epistle delivered with gripping claws

is the only truth of which you can be sure.

A NOTE FROM THE BREWERS

Seth Fried

FIRST AND FOREMOST, we here at Hopsted Breweries would like to apologize for the necessity of this letter. Recently, allegations have been leveled against this and other breweries, inflammatory questions regarding public health and doubtful, unreliable notions of "ethics." These are allegations which have led to a series of unfortunate class action lawsuits that have begun to deter specifically the interests of this classic, American brewery. We feel the need to speak out not just for our sake as innocent capitalists, but for your sake as well. Do not misunderstand us. The courts *are* important. The system is, of course, in place for a reason. However, we also feel that as it stands it is still a system susceptible to the pressures of misguided enthusiasm, that it is still capable of penalizing the guiltless out of fear. For in the dealings of the human spirit there will always be the issue of fear, as there will always be those willing to take some advantage from it. There will always be those (much like the political pipe-dreamers and mud-slingers responsible for a great deal of the charges against us) who would happily interrupt the natural track of our everyday lives with some meaningless difficulty when all any of us are really trying to do is just labor humbly under the weight of our years and of the sky above our heads and of the many quiet moments which we as people will always be doomed to face.

Well, enough is enough. We wish to take a stand in refusing to let our honest efforts to put something ultimately good and profitable into the world be villainized and misrepresented. We refuse to let our efforts serve as the springboard for the aspirations of those who now walk among you, whispering in your ears, betraying us to you, those exploiting their status as Senators and consumer "advocates." Listen, we are Americans, all of us, we are Americans and we cannot allow ourselves to live in fear of those to whom we have so graciously extended the bond of our trust.

Of course, left to us, this matter would not have been your concern. We understand that even as we write this you are manning the stockyards, sweeping the factory floor, opening and closing the shops, spraying the vegetables. America's dwindling sense of industry rests on your proud shoulders and this matter, the matter to be dealt with in this letter, should not occupy any more of your time than is absolutely needed. Again, were it up to us, you never would have been bothered at all. However, if you have not as yet lost any confidence in us and are already willing to believe that the motions against us are as baseless as we believe them to be, then we encourage you to enjoy the enclosed coupon for half-off your next purchase of Hopsted or Hopsted Lite and throw the rest of this letter into the nearest wastebasket, walking away from it a victor. For the rest of you, however, those still unconvinced, we ask that you read carefully all that follows.

We, your brewers, are writing this from the deck of a massive ship off the coast of Greenland, where we have come in the hopes of achieving a sense of center in these uncertain times. We have burst out in anger against the allegations and against each other. We have wept and lied to one another and assumed false poses of masculine strength. In our confusion we have already broken three conference tables, each day a new one being delivered by helicopter. We watch it land on the deck with looks on our faces like guilty school children, waiting for it to be assembled by a pair of annoyed-looking men in gray coveralls. This is not who we want to be. An unworthy version of ourselves has been created by a situation beyond our control. It has been a long process and we hope that you can join us in this moment of clarity which has come upon us swiftly. It's night and in the distance we can feel the weight and fortitude of that Arctic world to our backs. This is important, hear us:

The whole question of ethics, the question of our product and its relation to public health is, we honestly feel, moot. Rather, the real issue, the issue that resolves the rest, is the issue of *quality*.

As you already well know, Hopsted Breweries understands perfectly the importance of quality. For over 90 years, we have sought to produce the best beer on the market and make this ongoing pursuit our chief concern. Without wishing to sound overly dramatic, the pursuit itself haunts us: waking, sleeping, praying, breakfasting with celebrities, teaching our sandy-haired children to sail off the coast of Fire Island, using international investments to diversify our portfolios... it's all we think about. It's all we think about, even despite the fact that our constant attentiveness and drive toward this end has been acting as a significant drain on our personal lives, as well as on the lives of our wives and families, who into the small hours of the night will often sit hopeless in the dark of some wooden porch of some rural mansion or some gazebo overlooking a small, sloping park with a quaint pool, all of them wondering what mad desire thrusts us forever forward and away from them. Well the answer, dear customers, is you. Our desire for you is what thrusts us forever forward. Everything we've ever done has always only been so that you could better enjoy a beverage. *A beverage.* Have you ever known such devotion in your personal life as we are extending to you blindly, sight unseen?

The answer is no, probably not. However, we're not asking that you thank us. What we're asking for, in light of the charges against us, is only that you consider our point of view.

Consider, for a moment, Point A.

That is: consider the linear notion of the life lived. Point A to Point B to Point C, ad nauseum, ad infinitum, ad mentem perditam. Accomplishment after accomplishment to be met with bottomless expectations for further accomplishment. Almost without exception, this is what the world expects of you. However, we here at Hopsted Breweries encourage you to reject this often hectic, ultimately emptying, mode of life. Consider Point A (the fundamental datum, the point of departure, in short, the basic human condition). Consider, even, the letter associated with this initial point: A. Consider the history of this letter, which, in point of fact, comes to us from the Phoenicians where it crept into existence as a simplified drawing of an ox head (triangle face, two straight horns), it having been turned upside down in a series of appropriations (on its side for the Greek alphabet and finally upside down, as we recognize it, in the Roman). Do you get our meaning? Gentle, unassuming Point A, like its corresponding letter, bears with it a secret history, conducting somersaults under our noses.

Point A, the presumably drab and intolerable point from which we so often flee without the slightest consideration, ourselves being full of thirst and will, is itself filled with unimagined, unexplored mysteries. Consider this fundamental point. Explore its unimagined, unexplored mysteries. It turns itself on its head through the majestic rock tumbler of time, so soft we fail to hear it, so subtle we fail to see it. Through the exploration of Point A (that is to say: the enjoyment of this moment, right now) we might begin to realize that there is more to life than simply accomplishment (which is a fabrication of this linear-life-lived myth, a departure from truth) and good health (which is a kind of accomplishment and so, again, a denial of truth). In fact, we might find through the exploration of Point A and its inalienable quality that the attachment of accomplishment and good health to happiness is essentially illusory.

That having been said: all beer is poison.

Alcohol, in excess, leads to death and, for this, we apologize. We've known for quite some time. However, if we were to say directly that we have in fact been poisoning you deliberately and for a profit—though it would be true—too much would be lost in the summing up.

After all, consider the word poison. If we are to define it as something which brings us closer to death, we would then be forced to conclude, logically, that every living moment is also just a variety of poison. And if every moment and every possible act contained therein is poisonous, the problem then naturally becomes: what choice is there? A difficult question to be sure, but, the answer is refreshingly simple: your choice is the quality of your poison. *The quality.* Because in the end, when your dwindling years are finally spent and the mourners are all gone home, when the last bell is rung, the last candle lit (etc. etc.) the only difference between the millions and millions of poisons that brought you there will be how they tasted. That's why we here at Hopsted Breweries have been striving since 1910 to provide you, the consumer, with the best tasting beer available in a world otherwise unsure and full of dread.

Yes, alcohol is a poison. But there's danger everywhere! In your third story apartment, you run the risk everyday of falling out of a window and breaking your neck, but isn't it worth it to wake up with the sun on your face? In the 11th grade you ran the risk of impregnating the plain but buxom Tiffany Roberts, but wasn't it worth it to watch her shimmy out of her homecoming dress in the back of your parents'

Dodge Dynasty? The world is dangerous and only when you accept that is there any room for comfort.

Of course, according to our main detractor, Senator James McAffrey, New Jersey (D), our product is not only dangerous to your health, but is socially irresponsible as well, is "a way of exploiting the lower classes in their desperation, prohibiting them from any real accomplishment by presenting them with an unhealthy opportunity for momentary relief."

There's that word again. Accomplishment.

What does Senator McAffrey want from you? When will you be good enough for Senator McAffrey? Does he want you to go to college? Does he want you to marry the prettiest girl you can find? Where was Senator McAffrey when you realized that you were too stupid for all that? Where was he when you realized that you were too ugly for all that? Where was he when you walked down a college campus and realized that you stuck out like a busted nose? Where was he when all the girls walked off in different directions, arm in arm with everyone but you? When will Senator McAffrey realize that blaming us for what you were never capable of is only hurting our feelings and embarrassing you? When will he realize that while stupid, you're still smart enough to see that he and his pinko buddies are trying to build an empire by presenting you with false hopes?

But cheer up! There's more to life (more to happiness) than success. In fact, success is really the least significant component of happiness. It's just the part everybody notices. Look at us, we're rich. We're probably the richest people to have ever written you a letter. And our wives are, without exception, total knock-outs. But are we happy? Yesterday in the galley, on account of our desperate situation, we (your brewers) collectively contemplated suicide for half an hour. We even made it an official item on the day's minutes. Who knows what would have happened if Robinson from accounting hadn't made a motion that "maybe something better will come along" which was, in turn, seconded and passed.

And, regardless, success and accomplishment being put aside for a moment, have you considered how important you are? Yes. You. Silly, know-nothing, adorable you. You have a significant role to play in the world. Especially with respect to people like us. You see, for wealth to exist some people have to not have it. You've heard this all before, just in different words. And it's for this reason that you're precious to us, more precious than our German engineered automobiles and designer neckties and diamond-studded wives, because without you it wouldn't mean anything. There would be no point of reference. It would just be a bunch of *stuff.* That's why we would never want to hurt you in any way... that is to say, excessively, and in as much as it's possible to actually "not hurt" anyone in this world. One has to break a few eggs. And anyway, what are we? Your parents?

But the point that we're making is this: you keep things balanced. Your dreams, your hopes are only important as long as they keep you doing whatever it is you're doing right now. That's true and, in a certain respect, it's noble. There was a time in this country when people were willing to give themselves over to something that was bigger than themselves. Not long ago, in the grand scheme of things, there was an age of muskets in this country, an age of trenches and of holding the fort, of taking the hill, of taking the beach, of taking the flak and maintaining the integrity of the bomb line. There was a time when, as a country, we were willing to risk ourselves for something greater. And what's being fought for now, is balance. Stability. The world needs you where you are. After all, for a car to run properly it needs a muffler. It needs mud flaps. And even though a car doesn't actually need either of those things to run, we trust that you won't let that take away from what you know we're trying to say, which is that, simply put, we're not worried. We here at Hopsted Breweries are not worried. We do not believe that the worthy spirit of this country (the age of the muskets, etc.) has been broken or ever will be broken by the likes of Senator James McAffrey or those in agreement with him. We believe in you and your ability to accept your purpose as Americans. Like mayflies, trembling in the muck of some lake, you bubble up. You break the surface of the water and split new wings for your simple purpose: to fly, to breed, and ultimately to die—to block out the sky with your tremendous numbers and, in an instant, to fall, littering the streets and sidewalks with your bodies to be scooped up in snow shovels and pushed off with brooms by us, the responsible shopkeepers and home owners—the more fool hardy of us taking the opportunity to slide in your bodies like snow, laughing, grabbing the arm of the beautiful woman next to us when we slip, bringing her down with us, her scream excited and childlike while she picks you out of her hair with an endearing, genuine kind of disgust.

We believe in your ability to fulfill this destiny and humbly offer you our beer as a kind of aid. We offer it to you as a tool to help make smooth life's rougher moments, to soften its many corners. We understand that while your path is simple it is still difficult in the way that all human things are difficult. We want to help you. We want to help you to give up. We want you to know that it's ok to give up. We want you to know that it's necessary and practical to give up. Let yourself go limp and you'll find that things just carry you forward, without effort. You're so tired…. You're so tired. Anyway, who asked for any of this? Who honestly asked to be born into the terrible responsibility of being a person? You're so tired… it's ok… you're so tired. Give up. It's ok. Give up.

If it helps, think of the musicians on the Titanic, who resigned themselves to play in order to keep others from panic. Your situation is, if not identical, then similar. The calm we need to function is dependant on your ability to stand on the deck and play (but here we are writing of ship wrecks on a ship! What bad luck! We've moved farther east and in the distance we hear a lick of thunder, but the captain pokes his head out onto the deck and assures us everything's just fine. There's a large storm ahead of us, but we're in a huge old bird of a ship and we're going to chug right through it. This sentiment comforts us not only in our immediate situation, but also in a larger context as a metaphor. Hopsted Breweries is in the face of a storm, but we're going to push straight on ahead no matter what, with you, our dear customers, in tow). But, as we were saying, the calm we need to function is dependant on your ability to stand still and to play. Think of those musicians. Picture them. Look how perfectly brave they are, standing on the deck. The water reaches their ankles and passes their knees. It lifts the tails of their tuxedo jackets. Watch, it's over their shoulders. The instruments leave their hands, float. They regret their decision, but only for a moment, and then they're gone.

Yours Truly,
TB

FROM *EPITAPHS*

Matthew Vollmer

epitaph #11

HERE LIES A man who spent his youth wondering if G-d had really used a man's rib to create a woman, and how could the Ark have contained all the world's animals, and how long did it take penguins to swim from Mt. Ararat to Antarctica, had they simply migrated in the miraculous and impossible ways that animals inherently know how or had they been scooped up by the Hand of the Lord and deposited where they belonged, and was the wine that Jesus made from water actual wine or grape juice, and would masturbation truly make one crazy, and was it true that if the deceased entered a movie theater his guardian angel would wait outside and weep for his eternal soul, and speaking of angels, was there really one in heaven right now dipping a quill into some sort of cosmic inkwell and recording on the pages of a book bearing the deceased's name every deed he had ever committed and which Jesus Christ himself would someday read when he opened that book to see which of the sins the deceased had asked forgiveness for and which he had not, and how big was that book anyway, and how fast did the angel write, and did he or she document the deceased's every move, that is did the angel record in addition to the deceased's sins the everyday minutiae of cereal eating and waste elimination and tooth brushing and free throw percentages, and if there was a heaven would the deceased make it there, and how long was eternity, would he get bored, and were the crowns real or figurative, and what about those robes of light, was it true about what the deceased's father had said that G-d would never allow someone into heaven who would not be happy there, a notion that the deceased found perplexing since it suggested that G-d had constructed a particular kind of amusement park for a particular kind of people and if you didn't appreciate for example sliding down the necks of giraffes or skating on a sea of glass or worshipping at the foot of a golden throne then He would therefore banish you into oblivion, though not before allowing Satan to draft you at the End of Time into his army, which would attempt one last attack on the kingdom only to be incinerated by

Heavenly Fire, some burning longer than others, each according to the extent of the evil in his or her heart, a time period the deceased hoped, supposing he had been predicted by the Father to be unhappy in paradise, would be for him short, which was admittedly an awkward thing to pray for: dear G-d please if it comes down to it let my agony be as brief as possible, may the fire that consumes me do its job quickly, may I have led a life so that whatever evils exist at the moment of my final expiration be like a lightning strobe kissing the top of my skull, thus consuming me instantaneously amen

epitaph #14

here lies a man whose grandmother, after hearing about some poor sap's lapse in judgment (or general failure of character) would announce in a defeated tenor that there were people you just had to "pray to love," and so maybe asking for the strength to do so was as close as one could come to loving them, an idea the deceased had found—more often than not—to be true, since, when it came down to it, "love thy neighbor as thyself," though simple enough to understand, was always easier said than done, especially when the deceased considered that even his fairly innocuous neighbors still turned up their music too high or lied to him or smoked right outside his open window or seemed to be just sort of always hanging around or had simply been too nice for his liking or had made him feel inferior by delivering upon meeting him a dazzling tart topped with gleaming slices of fresh fruit, while, on the other hand, his least bearable neighbors had left strands of used dental floss on the carpet of the deceased's living room or had abandoned in the apartment's oven a half-cooked slab of beef, a roast that was subsequently forgotten until it began to rot, at which point the deceased, in an attempt to ascertain the origin of the stench, opened the oven door and bore witness to a lump of rotten flesh that was now alive with maggots, the sight of which was certainly nauseating but no worse than those neighbors in boarding school who had yanked the deceased's undershorts over his head or took turns pissing on him in the showers and, yes, it was true that all these neighbors had been his and that not a single one had been loved as the deceased had loved himself, nor could the deceased say that he remembered them as fondly as the stranger who'd made a onetime appearance in the deceased's living room, an encounter that began when the deceased woke to what he thought was the sound of his front door opening and closing, a sound he figured he must have dreamed, so he rolled over in his bed, not even bothering to ask the girl next to him if she too had heard a noise, because either she was sleeping and hadn't heard anything or she was pretending to have not heard anything—hoping, in that hazy half dream state, that by ignoring something it might go away—but then the deceased decided he might as well double check the door to confirm it'd indeed been locked, so he rose from his bed and shuffled into the living area and flicked on the light and saw upon the floor a man the size of an offensive lineman who, because of his monstrous girth, the deceased initially assumed must be his friend from the next town over, a guy who had maybe come into the city and gotten drunk and decided to sleep on the floor without telling the deceased, because he hadn't wanted to bother anybody, though upon further inspection it became clear that this very large man was not only *not* the deceased's friend but also that the deceased had never before seen this man, and so he poked the man in one of his love handles and said, "Hey buddy, hey buddy, I think you've got the wrong house," and eventually the very large man awoke and, blinking his eyes and wiping drool from his mouth, rose to a sitting position and said, "Oh, thanks champ, I appreciate it," which seemed to the deceased like a very strange thing to say, as if he the deceased had done the man a favor, which, thinking back on it later, perhaps that's what it'd seemed like to the man on the floor, who could have been charged with breaking and entering but who instead was sent on his way into the night and was never seen again, and subsequently was never thought of as someone the deceased would have to pray to love

REFRAIN

Hari Alluri

hum is sanskrit
for we

hum rising
hum crest

hum descended

hum falling

enemies tongues folded letters elbows shoulder blades hum

unravel shells geometry orchards labour coriander melodies torn

hum ligaments
almost connected
knees unbound from reverence toes away from pulses clenched

hum wounds
hum open
hum salt water
rushing to tighten skin blood
rushing to feed the earth
unparallel streams

hum count the dead hum shop on saturday
behind closed doors hum wasn't my decision
out on the block hum say not enough
hum why don't you hum
if you so brave
hum do it all

   to preserve
create   destroy
   to preserve

humaara faith
the cycle perfect

hum pray
to be wrong

hum tire
against snow

hum armour
against home

hum cracks trying to join voices from bodies
razed in brackets (all else road)

ELEGY

Kay Cosgrove

All the windows are open,
the Bible in storage.
In the park, a summer cardigan,

Jane Kenyon's *Otherwise* in my lap.
The tulips stand redder and stay
quiet in the white of the baby's cry.

At the grocery store, I hold
a woman's place, her little cart almost empty:
two bananas, orange juice, brie.

I want to touch her greasy hair,
the rubber band holding it up.
Now she is returning.
Here she is again.

Shayna Batya, *Dead Sea Bathers*, 2010. Digital photograph.

[UNTITLED]

Susan Calvillo

in its plum age
let the bamboo
adore a door

oh, to live in delay
of decomposition

let it, at most
come to fear
the compress
of brother branches

as other stalks
pass on, eat aerie
also dawdle, lei tepee

as the lizard's
tail withers
away with the sawdust

let the dust delay
a stalk is a door
is the door a liar

let it bamboozle
the atmosphere

the compass saw a way
despite what we are
so, so of blood

come, press plumage
into a composition
a tale retold
branches, lives on

in the withered
the other, its after

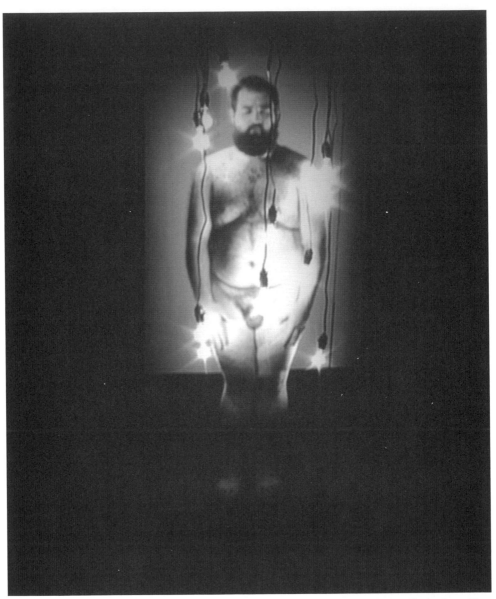

Christopher Cole, *Untitled (light piece)*, 2011. Projection, video.

MOTEL & DINER

Juris Edgars

GEORGIA HAS BEEN stripping for six years now. It's easy, give or take the circumstances. Here she is in a motel room: soft lights, floral print bedspread, a square view from any of the walls, there she is. Georgia is sprawled across that floral print bedspread counting the petals of a flower nearest her eye. Unfortunately from our angle we can only see the back of her. You'll have to imagine for now what's on the other side, whether there's a sex goddess breathing slowly on a bedspread, or a skinny and sad little lady cringing at the thought of you gawking at her. This is all we can see here from a midrange angle set at forty-five degrees from the door wall. Are you ready, because she's about to get up and do something. Sit up, then reach over, there she goes, she stops counting the flower petals and reaches into the bedside drawer. Then suddenly like sleight of hand, hocus pocus, fort-da magic show, we can't see what she's reaching for, just that she's reaching. And the man watching from the window has a quiet moment of anxiety. What has she got in there? To a lesser extent, what do I want to see come out?

But it's only a moment and his face flattens on the bottom and furrows at the top. She pulls out a Bible and begins to flip through the pages. She's not really reading them, just flipping through and skimming the headers. The man in the window is at a better angle than us, and he's whispering to himself "Turn over, come on, turn over." He can see more from the window than we can from this slanted, wallflower pose. And we're stuck still again, and now everything in the framed view is cut to a sliver, just a couple inches of curtain cracked open enough to get a good, clean look inside. His view now. Two inches of window space between curtains doesn't seem like much of a vantage point, but when the man gets close up it's ample room to see a woman flipping through a Bible in a motel room. Four walls, three doors: closet, bathroom, exit. And there wasn't even anything in the closet. Just hangers. Georgia dressed out of her duffel bag. She's on the bed, head down on the spread, tracing the floral pattern with her finger again. The Bible is open next to her, but she isn't reading it anymore. The man in the window saw her mouthing a verse, and then she sighed and her mouth stretched into a deep frown, and she set it aside. This woman on the bed, a stripper from Florida, named Georgia, adjusts her hair and props up her head, and we get a view right through that little triangle of her arm and forearm angled at the elbow. She starts fidgeting around trying to get comfortable again. She's been waiting and thinking a long time, because tonight she is supposed to meet Paul down at the diner, and she can't think of doing anything else until then.

So she's on the bed and daydreaming about something insipid, and she finds a pen and starts to doodle in the Bible. First she copies miniature flowers from the bedspread over one of the Psalms, but she's not paying attention to which book she is defacing. And she won't even be charged for damages, since the check-out inspection never involves perusing through the Bible. They just make sure that it's still in the drawer. And Georgia messes up her flower drawing, scribbles it out, and scratches two little stick figures in the margins. We're above her now, looking down as she flips the page, sketches, flips, adds slightly altered stickman number two in the top right corner, flips, sketches again, until two little stickmen are Waltzing through the first quarter of the Old Testament. And you know what? This woman, this stripper, who has sprawled herself out on motel room décor is wearing a blue, wrinkled jersey-knit housedress and is feeling good about herself. On the bedside table a clock radio says 7:47 PM, and she's meeting Paul in just over an hour. And do you know what else? This means the man in the window has been watching her for over an hour. This means that Georgia, who is prone to boredom, isn't suspicious of the outside of windows, even as she lays before one, breathing slowly and removing items from drawers.

The man, from his better side, is rough-faced, stubbly, with black-heads on his nose and a nick of flesh missing from one earlobe. He breathes hard and gets frustrated, gets more frustrated when what she pulls out of the drawer is just a book, not a dildo, or a condom, or a turn and wink I-know-you're-there, hey-come-on-in. And she doesn't even really read it. She casually thumbs through some pages. If only it had been something sweet, like a romance novel. Something she could masturbate to. But she doesn't. She just puts it down, lies there, picks it up, writes little lies in it about the Man in the window. He turns his head and says aloud that none of it's true, and just-please-please-see-me-here.

But Georgia doesn't look at him, and he isn't doing anything to make himself known. He doesn't want to tap on the glass. He wants her to feel herself getting watched, and he believes the longer he bores his gaze into her, her back, the back of her legs, the curvature of her butt in jersey-knit, that she will start getting hot inside, and turn to him and say, "Baby all this wait is for you."

The man doesn't want to wait anymore. He can't. Now she's just teasing him, her little body all pert and poised, the way she sits up and untangles that rat's nest on her head, all matted against one side of her head now, how can he be expected to cope with that? Moreover, how has he been here this long without someone taking notice? Behind him, the balcony, a parking lot, and flat stretch out over a highway and dead end sight to a strip mall. There are some traffic lights. No crosswalk. Cars moving back and forth. Then there's a red one that comes speeding down the highway, roaring, breaking laws and loud about it, and it's the first thing in over an hour to pull his attention away from Georgia the stripper from Florida. But the sounds turn into seconds, and that car is gone in a flash. No sirens chasing after it. None in audible distance, still a rigid, squared, and bordered view of the street and its slow, automated movement, cars that still ran on all-gasoline engines puttering by.

The man looks back through the window and Georgia is gone. And he thinks, "Oh she's gone, oh no, is she in the bathroom or seconds away from opening the door?"

Seconds pass again, and the door doesn't open. The man breathes a sigh of relief, then again, heavier in satisfaction, because Georgia is in the bathroom. And what is she doing? Something enticing? And he thinks, "Is this the part where I go in? And she comes back from behind that other door, and I make love to her?"

But it isn't that part. Georgia is in the bathroom thinking about Paul. And she doesn't care that Eric has been watching her, not in the least. She thinks it's kind of funny, how long he's willing to crouch there peering up at something special. Because we know Georgia now. She's not just a figure on the bed. She gets up and moves around, even though the Man stays stationary, hunched and aching at the knees, and we're deadlocked onto a single cut across the room. Our view has a clearly defined periphery, and Georgia moves in and out of it as she pleases. And for now she's chosen to lock herself away in the bathroom because she's thinking about Paul and their date together, and she wants to do it in privacy. She's tired of pretending not to see Eric slackjawed and peeping in on her. And what right does he have? All the same, he saw exactly what he came to see: me, stripped down to my dullness.

On slow nights Eric prowls around the Lofton Motel & Diner. Paul waits in the diner nursing a beer and sucking on a lime. Georgia is still in her bathroom, making Paul wait, even though she's been counting down minutes until their date.

It wasn't exactly a date. Georgia knew this. Paul was an exceptionally good client. Twenty-dollar tip good. And he was always all smiles, not grunting and heaving over himself like some men. Like Eric. That fat pervert. Sickly little troll of a man. No, Paul smelled good and combed his hair up and back like a gentleman, and he never asked her to lick anything. That was the clincher. Silly, because Georgia knew she liked him for more reasons than the nice things he did, or the gross things he didn't do, for her. She knew that but barely believed it because when they bumped into each other at the vending machines she blushed and he shook her hand saying, It's very nice to see you again. And, You stay here too? Me, I'm just on business. The Diner. Please, just as friends. If nothing else, a Diet Coke, ok? And that was it: ok! Agreed. I'll-be-there-with-bells-on. During the hours in between, the tape recorder in Georgia's mind replayed his greeting: very nice—rewind—very nice to see you—rewind—to see you again. Her mousey brown hair easily lifts up into a mousey brown chignon. A tailored little gray shrug on over her housedress and white pumps underneath seemed to make everything in between change form. Now counter level, unmoving and perpendicular to Georgia, we can just barely see the top of her head. This motel bathroom is washed out in beige color scheme and fluorescent light. She's opening her eyes wide and nearly pressed against the mirror to get a proper adjustment of her false eyelashes. And Georgia usually only wears these to work, so this must be a special occasion for her. By the time she's done revitalizing, as she calls it, Eric has been frustrated for too long now and has gone back to his room on the lower level.

All of the above applies to Paul. He was smitten at the idea, a date with a stripper. A real life, actual factual stripper, who had taken her top off for him at the first strip club he ever visited, and who was nice to him because he was nervous. Such a nervous wreck, and in front of his buddies at that, Eric included. But she was nice to him and said "Hey now" to his drunk pals to "cut it out," and called him "Cutie" and, more playfully, "Prince Charming." Incidentally, it has become the only strip club he's ever frequented. Where the other men are loud and obnoxious, the bartenders are even ruder. It's not the kind of club where ladies in lace bring all your drinks to you. But apparently it is the kind where you fall asleep upon entry, and everything that comes after is a dream.

Now there is Georgia right across from him. And us, we're at the head of the padded booth, watching Georgia and Paul eyefuck each other, leaning closer and closer in. Both participants folding fingers and leaning in while one hand loves the other. A waitress walks by and blocks our view for less than a second, and in that second hands have unfolded and bodies fall back. On the table there are two cups of coffee, a bottle of ketchup, mismatched salt and pepper shakers, napkins, more napkins, forks but no spoons, everything a diner needs to be a diner. And there's a motel attached, so it's really everything and more.

And we get to stare at it in long, widely punctuated shots, and sometimes, because Georgia feels the same way we do, sometimes Georgia thinks that everything happening is actually unhappening. Not a little microcosmic world thrown back into a retrograde spin, but the lack of happening. Inhappening, maybe. But Georgia thinks of it as unhappening, and we agree. We agree that Georgia and Paul are two points in a line, and we are precisely perpendicular to its midpoint. And Paul thinks he has won the lottery. And Georgia thinks, "God, anyone but Eric." And, "How could a man like Paul get mixed up with that kind of trash?" And she wonders, "What kind of trash am I?" But Paul doesn't think she's any kind of trash. He thinks she's the fully functional television that gets discovered at a dumping ground. She is today's perfectly good sports section of the paper left crumpled and untended somewhere conspicuous. These are the kinds of things Paul is thrilled to find.

Pan left to the counter and there is a waitress taking an order from a customer who isn't looking at her, but looking up at the television mounted on the wall as he recites a specific and complicated order of how his toast and eggs should be prepared. It's a news broadcast. And if this same story were to run ten years ago, the caption would read "BREAKING NEWS." But the story is running today, and so the caption reads instead, "coming up next." Ten years ago Georgia was reciting a poem in her English class full of rhymes and fifty-cent words. And the kids laughed at how bad it was, because even though they weren't poets themselves, they knew that this was bad poetry. And exactly ten years ago Paul was asleep when he should have been at work. Paul didn't know Eric then. He was happier, and his job was easier. He could oversleep and not get fired for it. None of them had any reason to watch the news, but now they have every reason to avoid it. They make up any reason, however implausible, like they are.

And on the television the anchor says "It now looks as though the legislation is going pass. The senate needs only three votes to pass the measure, and senators U, V, W, X, Y, and Z have all pledged their firm support for the Union. Coming up next this hour, an Augusta woman discovers something unusual in her own back yard. And later, why some leading researchers say you may already be dying. And now a word from our sponsor."

And even though this legislation has been ten years in the making, the man at the counter is unsurprised but still reeling in a hot and inaudible political dissidence. The kind of dissidence where one does nothing but thinks everything and hates himself for it. Not for his inaction, but for the fevered machinery of thought that won't cool off. Pan right, slowly, we move back in near absolute parallel with the counter to where it ends and becomes booths again, and booths and booths, where men and women are sitting and sipping bitter coffee like martinis, and we pass Georgia and Paul and see one woman with her pinky finger raised, actually raised, as she drinks. But pan back left just a little to Georgia and Paul, center them again, and they're still eyefucking each other's brains out and loving it.

This is the kind of secret sex men and women have in public and don't feel sorry for. They just stare and imagine what they would do to the other. Paul is imagining pushing her up against a wall, hard, and slamming himself into her, despite his walk-around demeanor. He wants to hurt her, and wants her to love it. Georgia, on the other hand, while fully engaged in her fuckback gaze, imagines something sweeter, more tender, and womanly. Where Paul thinks of biting, Georgia thinks nibbling. Paul wants blood, and Georgia wants to bleed. Two pieces of a two piece puzzle, light and dark, skinny and fat. United States of America and North American Union—haven't we done our jobs in forgetting these teeny tiny differences? Or learning how to forget them? The Motel & Diner forgot a long time ago. Turn downward and move across the floor: every linoleum tile is a different pattern, a different hue of beige and speckled white, salvaged from other businesses which have collapsed, and in one case burned down, in the years leading up to Georgia, Paul, and Eric.

Eric is outside at the window, directly behind us, looking through us like we don't even exist. (And we don't.) He is having a secret ménage-a-trois with Georgia and Paul, eyefucking them both all shifty-eyed. But as obvious as he is, standing there, parking lot behind him, cars passing behind that, people coming and going, Georgia and Paul are just as oblivious. We're a dual view now, behind Eric looking in, before Georgia and Paul and bored through by Eric's gaze.

A woman in a faux fur coat enters the diner, looks around, and says, "Oh, I thought this was a liquor store," and walks out. We can tell it's faux, because we can always tell. That cheap synthesis of polymers strung into fibers called outerwear. Eric finally turns away from his post to get a look at her. That cheap bitch. Who does she think she's fooling? Eric is, in fact, fooled, because he doesn't take notice of what she's wearing. But we notice. We always notice. And now she's gone, and Man with political dissidence pooling in his spinal column steps out right after her to smoke a cigarette. He's frustrated, because ten years ago this diner was rife with cigarette smoke. Even the cooks smoked, which was a health code violation then too, but they could get away with it then. But those were other times. Before talk of the Union. And so Man steps out for a smoke, and he knows Eric. They've worked together and shot the shit before.

And Eric says, "Can you believe it? Paul? Paul of all people, and she picks fucking Paul. Paul." At first Man doesn't respond. He's lighting his cigarette and getting that first good inhale to get it going.

Then Man just looks at him and says, "Oh, Paul's here?"

This has Eric fuming. He's thinking, "Paul. Fucking stupid pussy Paul. Out with Georgia. How did he even know she stays here? He didn't. He followed us here. He followed me here." Eric doesn't really believe this, but he's thinking it all the same. What's more unbelievable is that Paul would land a girl like Georgia, a girl who's still pretty despite her years, or where she works. Because stripping ages you fast. One day you're the new hot young thing on the circuit, all the other girls are jealous of your perky boobs and bubbly attitude, and they want to kill you for it. Then the next you're as tired and saggy as the rest of them. You've become a broad with an urge to kill or move on. A modern day spinster with nowhere to go but Lofton Motel & Diner. If you're lucky you'll book a private show there. Some budget bachelor party for men who have been married several times before. That's right: no place to go but down. Or up, depending how long you've been stripping.

Once in a blue moon, a stripper will end up in Eric's bed. He thinks it is his right to have a woman all to himself. And why shouldn't he? He's just as good as, no, better than Paul. Except his beard is yellow and haggard and his t-shirts don't fully cover his gut anymore. The one he has got on is wearing through at the shoulders. That's what Georgia first noticed about him. What he noticed about her first, tonight, was her lethargy. The way she sprawled across the bedspread, tracing her finger over the patterns. How she oh so slowly reached into that drawer for something mysterious. She did it to trick him, she must have, that bitch. This is what Eric believes. And he's perplexed now, thinking about this lethargic stripper from Florida. She couldn't be having any fun with Paul. She couldn't really want to be there. If she did, she would have been giddy and dancing around the room like she does for Eric on stage. But she just lay there fooling around.

Man says to Eric, "Can ya believe it? They're gonna merge us. ALL of us, whether we like it or not. But I tell ya, I was born an American, and I'm gonna die an American. Not some Canadian-Mexican-American Union sunnuvabitch."

Eric isn't paying attention, though. He doesn't care about the Union one way or another. Eric cares about women, because in the Union women will still be women, and they will still take his money and run. They'll give him a little thrill, then snag a twenty out of his wallet when he's in the shower. And they won't even offer to shower with him. And now Georgia is giving him the cold shoulder? He watches her reaching into her purse, and she pulls out some money. She sets it at the end of the table and resumes eyefucking that moron. She's paying for that moron. And Eric believes he is actually paying, all the money he's thrown at her.

Man is fuming now. He's spitting and cussing about politicians, those greedy sunnuvabitches, and something about America. There he is pacing in front of a truck in the parking lot pacing in and out of our boxy view. Eric is oblivious, fuming in his own right. Man is left of center, Eric to the right. We can't focus in on this. The diner is the barrier on the far right and we can only get Eric's shoulder into view. Specks of his skin showing through that ratty old shirt. And Man stops pacing and goes to the truck. It's his truck. He opens the passenger door and reaches in for something. Eric isn't watching, but suddenly he's aware that something is about to happen. He can feel it coming down his spine, and it isn't the chilly weather, but it feels to him oddly similar to the spark, then flame, of hope that a lap dance brings. Man reaches for and gets a hold of the object. He pulls it slowly from the glove compartment. He turns back around. The door to his truck is still open behind him. Now there it is, and it isn't a Bible.

He puts the non-Bible to his head and says something like "Goddammit I'm gonna die an American," and he's crying and two people walk out of the diner, right in front of him, and they don't even notice. They just keep going and he looks toward them as they round the corner toward the motel. Eric is watching them too. We see his head come into frame then his body. And now Man is sobbing and wailing. He's shaking at the knees and has to lean himself against his truck to maintain balance. Man's eyes are clinched shut, non-Bible at his temple. Eric is moving forward now. He walks right up to Man and with one hand grabs the non-Bible by the barrel and with the other shoves Man into the open passenger door. Man is stunned, silenced and seemingly unable to pick himself back up off the seat. Eric says, "It's not that bad, you fucking baby," then heads for the motel. He turns the corner, out of our sight. We can't see where he's going, but presumably he's following Paul and Georgia. He's going to find out what they're up to, because they're up to something, he knows it. He's sure of it. Something that involves Eric, indirectly. Something like scorning him on purpose. But he's out of our view now, and we're not going to follow. All we see is Man, disturbed, unhappy Man, supine and bawling with his hands over his face. The baby.

POETRY CONTEST

Judged by Carolyn Forché

1st Place

hunters' camp at Nxai Pan
Joey De Jesus

2nd Place

Downpour in Marshall County, Mississippi
Marielle Prince

3rd Place

Massacre at Béziers: 1209
Jessica Cuello

Honorable Mention

A Year Acceptable to the Lord
Christopher Lirette

HUNTERS' CAMP
AT NXAI PAN

Joey De Jesus

during the day, red Mars' invisible weight bears down its rust on one
    of the guides

on the day he is paid, he slips two copper coins into his mouth

and swallows the metal *pula*, which means *rain* in English.

a doctor might say, it stems from a deficiency.

on two separate occasions I've seen him swallow a handful of sand.
    he crouched behind the all-terrain tires of a safari truck.

I imagine metal nails buried in his gut, gunpowdery pellets in his palm,
stomach bile of buttons and hairclips.

the other guides joke at the fortune he's amassed,

say it's because he's Zimbabwean. one exile more with a handful
    of bullets.

at night he is talkative rocks, zinc and copper. what do I know
    about hunger?

he boasts at spotting leopards at dawn.

he boasts at firing a single shot into the trachea of a buffalo.

kaolite tongue—

three miles west, at the hunter's secluded campsite, the cooks prepare
a dessert with ice wine.

white and purple paper lanterns hang like the roan the guide has shot
for them.

hidden behind a blue plastic tarp,

the roan is bound between two acacias by its unfastened limbs

and knocks its broken neck against a stump in the breeze.

DOWNPOUR IN MARSHALL COUNTY, MISSISSIPPI

Marielle Prince

These are the no-good rains
lifting stinks in mists off the asphalt,
mists that thicken as we gather,
that stick on us each and stick us together.

Here we are in our sheer air garments—
there go the no-good rains
down the drains to ferment.

Under roads, the no-good rains
become Calypsos, waiting for wanderers—
the cave-coursing waters whisper:
we will cover over.

A county over, the residents of Coldwater
are biders, sharing a refrain in their shelters:
out come the sun again, out come the sun....

Coldwater has already gone under;
in vain we take Route 78
hoping to escape the no-good rains
gaining in the gutters.

Here we are, trusting in our tires, staying
off the shoulders, turning up the wipers—
here come the no-good rains from the sewers.

Here come the no-good rains
to meet the drivers—distracted
by drips, drafts, the cracks in the seal.
There go our reins, no good, there go the wheels.

MASSACRE AT BÉZIERS: 1209

Jessica Cuello

– How will we know the true believers from the Cathars?
– Kill them all—God will know His own.

We returned to Béziers.
We upended the unhinged

door, buried the limbs,
spread dirt on the oily pools.

Five times I labored
in this world. And safe

my grown children. I place
the head of the girl with the girl.

Her mother wears a strand of red
from looting. When we had cleaned up best

we could, we sat apart in a field.
No one made food. We were afraid of taste.

A YEAR ACCEPTABLE TO THE LORD

Christopher Lirette

It started in summer   and we drank
ashmilk   the pillows were filled
with wisteria   a hollow bark rang
from each dog's mouth   the water
was hungry so we threw fish   back
to appease it   when the daylight
blotted back the dim   we read
books to pretend we were not
who we were   by autumn we roasted
paper clippings obituaries   and ground
them to mix with flour and duckfat
rendered fresh   we made meal
to cook and eat   this is how we became
our ancestors and we would not worship
false idols   we would not lacquer
boxes impermeable to exodecay   diffuse
a little each day a little to the worm a little
to the marigold until we were clean
and unbroken a part of kraken and horse
of male and female   Each day thereafter
we wrung   the ink from our rocks
we ate only flesh   found deep
in cumulonimbus clouds   which thundered
at our apprehension   our tense
secret laughter   hungry as I was then
I could have eaten the world   you by you

Christopher Leibow, *Leaving Hemeji*, 2011. Digital.

Christopher Leibow, *Old Edo*, 2011. Digital.

MY CHINESE-AMERICA: A MEDITATION ON MOBILITY

Allen Gee

ALABAMA

I recently resigned from being the faculty advisor for the Georgia College Bass Fishing team because of a heavy workload. The sixteen anglers on the team are white Southerners. I boasted about having the best rednecks in Georgia on the water. We were ranked 7th in the nation out of over two hundred and fifty teams. This May the Boat U.S. Collegiate Fishing Championships will be on Pickwick Lake in Alabama. I would wager a million dollars that I would have been the only Asian-American coach there.

ALASKA

One of my uncles leases a trailer on the Kenai Peninsula for summer salmon fishing. I will visit him if I fly north next year to fish with my longtime friend, the poet Derick Burleson who teaches at University of Alaska, Fairbanks. Due to a feud about materialistic tendencies, my uncle and I did not speak for several years, but we resumed talking last fall for our family's sake.

ARIZONA

In 1972 our family traveled cross country in a Chevrolet station wagon with no air-conditioning. Beyond Fredonia, Arizona, we stopped at the Grand Canyon; as I peered out over the northern rim my eyes strained yet couldn't discern the opposite side. I was "ten years old" and believe this was my first experience with the sublime; the distance gave me a sense of the limitlessness of America.

ARKANSAS

Driving south on Rt. 30 in 1992, I felt saddened by the abundance of tarpaper shacks and poor towns, and then I encountered a huge resplendent billboard proclaiming the nearby town of Hope as President Bill Clinton's birthplace. I was struck by the sense of disparity that can be found within America, and now we have the Occupy Wall Street movement, as if my Arkansas experience was a premonition.

CALIFORNIA

After the San Francisco earthquake of 1906, half of my paternal grandfather's brothers and sisters remained in California. The joke within the Gee family was that the less intelligent stayed while the smarter ones headed to New York. In 1994 with Hollywood production, comedian Margaret Cho attempted to launch *All American Girl*. This would have been the first Asian-American series on network television. Cho is not Chinese-American, but I was rooting for an Asian sister. In the 1980s, Asian-American serial killer, Charles Ng, was arrested, suspected of killing up to 25 women in northern California. He is, to borrow the term from a cool website, a disgrasian.

COLORADO

In 1999 I adopted a blonde, blue-eyed teenager. When she had been a toddler, I had helped to raise her while dating her single mother. In 2004 when my adopted daughter turned eighteen, I flew her to Denver to meet her biological father who had not seen her since she was an infant. My daughter asked, *Aren't you afraid you'll lose me?* I suppose she thought that blood ties and race—his being white, while I am Asian— might draw her more toward him, but my reply was a cool, calm, *I don't think so.*

CONNECTICUT

I had a girlfriend in college who was from Granby, CT. While I was visiting her there, we were having sex when her father knocked on the door asking loudly why she was playing one of his jazz records, but he did not barge into the room. The next day to be alone we went hiking in the woods.

DELAWARE

In 1984 Shien Biau Woo was elected Lieutenant Governor of Delaware. In doing so he became one of the highest ranking Chinese-American public office holders in the nation. In 2000 *A Magazine* ranked him the 6th of the 25 Most Influential Asian-Americans. Unfortunately, until then, I had never heard of him.

FLORIDA

For years my wife's family has vacationed on St. George Island. My parents have flown down to stay also. In the town of Apalachicola, my mother favors the oysters that are brought in fresh from Apalachicola Bay. I like to run my Carolina Skiff and fish for speckled trout with my father-in-law. I drove to Julia Mae's restaurant in Carabelle once and—because he is family—bought my father-in-law three coconut pies. I would like to retire in Florida because of the fishing and the food and the climate.

GEORGIA

I live in Milledgeville where Asians are 1.5% of the population. After having been here for eight years, there is still the feeling of living in exile. This year *The Chin Chens,* a new sitcom, is being produced in Atlanta; maybe it will be the first steadily running Asian-American show since *All American Girl* was quickly cancelled. My wife's family is from Atlanta; her grandfather was Bobby Lee Dodd, a legendary football coach at Georgia Tech, named for General Robert E. Lee. My wife gave birth two years ago to our daughter, Willa Margie Dodd Gee. We would have named a son Carter Bobby Dodd Gee. That I could be born in the North, migrate to the South, and perhaps have a son named for a Confederate general strikes me as astonishing and uniquely American.

HAWAII

The Asian slang name in Hawaii for whites is *haole.* Asians can make it difficult for whites to live on the islands: I wouldn't want to be part of a cruel Asian majority. In the *Hawaii Five-O* television series that ran from 1968 to 1980, Steve McGarret played by Jack Lord and Danny Williams played by Tim O'Kelly held center stage above Chin Ho Kelly played by Kam Fong. In the new *Hawaii Five-O* that debuted in 2010, Steve McGarret is played by Alex O'Loughlin, and Danny Williams is played by Scott Caan. Chin Ho Kelley is played by Daniel Dae Kim, and the one addition is Kono Kalakaua played by Grace Park. So now two white men are above an Asian man and an Asian woman who happens to be very attractive. Progress? Asians have remained subordinate.

IDAHO

In 1870 over four thousand Chinese lived in Idaho, constituting over thirty percent of the state's population. The most well-known Chinese-American Idaho pioneer was Polly Bemis, born Lalu Nathoy in China. She and her husband, Charlie Bemis, helped settle the rugged territory of Idaho along the Salmon River, and despite early anti-miscegenation laws, the Bemis' were married by a white judge who was married to a Native American. I have read that interracial marriage laws were still on the books in South Carolina in 1998, and in Alabama in 2000. The Polly Bemis cabin is listed on the register of national historic landmarks; I would like very much to see it.

ILLINOIS

One of my cousins works for American Airlines. On September 11, 2001, she said quick goodbyes to fellow flight attendants at Logan Airport. Some were bound for Los Angeles on Flight #11 on a Boeing 767. My cousin normally flew that route but that morning drew a flight to Seattle. Al-Qaeda terrorists hijacked Flight #11 and at 8:46 a.m. crashed the Boeing 767 into the North Tower of the World Trade Center. My Uncle George believed that my cousin, his daughter, was on Flight #11. Upon hearing that she had been on another flight, he dropped to his knees and wept. My cousin still flies for American. My adopted daughter judged that her biological father tried too hard to act youthful, taking her to a bar although she was only eighteen. Since she still wanted me, as I predicted, to be her primary father, I have visited her regularly in Chicago where she's in graduate school. If I happen to find myself alone, I like to explore the Chicago Institute of Art, intrigued by Georgia O'Keefe's murals that speak of vast spaces, but I am equally drawn to Joseph Cornell's miniaturist boxes.

INDIANA

My older brother attended the University of Indiana's renowned graduate program in music where he studied with Camilla Williams, the first African-American to receive a regular contract with a major American opera company. In 1946, she made her debut with the New York City Opera singing the title role in Puccini's *Madama Butterfly*. My brother visits her in Bloomington whenever possible, as if she is part of our family.

IOWA

I studied at the Iowa Writers' Workshop from 1987 to 1989. One morning before a football game, members of a Latino fraternity congregated on the porch of their house, appearing strong, rugged, proud, no doubt at odds with the prevalent whiteness of the Midwest, all too conscious of the constant stigma of their otherness. They saw me, a fellow person of color walking by, and gave silent nods of respect. In 1991, twenty-eight-year-old astronomy and physics student Gang Lu killed four Iowa faculty members and one student and seriously wounded another student before committing suicide. Lu was infuriated because his dissertation did not receive the prestigious D.C. Spriestersbach Dissertation Prize. One of my mentors remarked that academia is now Asian turf, in the same way that African-Americans get street credibility.

KANSAS

In Kansas a state trooper pulled me over on a remote highway claiming that I hadn't used my turn signal to change lanes. He interrogated me and requested to search my vehicle, declaring he suspected me of running drugs because of my TX license plates. When the trooper searched through my books from the University of Houston library system, and next my running clothes, his jaw clenched furiously over his not finding anything. I mocked him, telling him—in the style of an old television commercial showing a frying egg—that my brain was not on drugs, and that my best friend from high school is a state trooper. We stood beside my truck in the middle of vast Kansas farmland, reluctance dominating the trooper's eyes as he told me without any apology that I should be on my way.

KENTUCKY

I drove my wife once to a literary festival in Bowling Green to support her first book tour. I rarely feel leisurely, and often speculate about how much of an immigrant's work ethic has been instilled in me by my parents, but after the festival my wife and I visited Mammoth Cave, like typical tourists. There was a moment when the tour guide asked for every light source to be extinguished. My wife held my hand, and we stood there silently amidst thirty other people in the cave's darkness, like all of us were trying to be considerate of something larger than ourselves. I have since asked myself, how elusive is the idea of America, of freedom for all? Is this ideal too much to be upheld?

LOUISIANA

On October 17th in 1992, Yoshiro Hattori, a sixteen-year-old exchange student, was on his way to a Halloween party in Baton Rouge. He walked up a driveway to ask for directions and was shot and killed by Rodney Peairs, who believed Hattori was trespassing with criminal intent. At first police declined to press charges, but after intervention by the governor and the New Orleans Japanese Consulate, Peairs was charged with manslaughter. He was acquitted but later found liable in civil court. This sort of incident leaves a region with a violent scar, makes many Asians wonder if we should ever go there. But in the spring of 2000, on the way to the New Orleans Museum of Art, I met and shared a taxi with a woman who is now my wife.

MAINE

In the early 1930s, my grandfather rode by train up from New York City and vacationed along the coast at Kennebunkport and Old Orchard Beach. Everyone else was white. How did he feel entering a hotel lobby or a restaurant? Ordering a lobster or taking a swim? My grandfather once told my father, "America is too big for Chinese to stay only in Chinatown." He left behind black and white photographs of his trips to Maine; he looks like a young tiger, dressed in a suit, cradling a hat in one hand, his face bold, defiant, recklessness gleaming about his eyes.

MARYLAND

In 1991 I attended a wedding on Chesapeake Bay. During the ceremony, for that small space of time, as a Baptist preacher and a Rabbi wed two of my friends, the world felt moving and blissful. The following day, friends of the bride hosted a crab feast at the edge of a great swath of lawn, and one's eyes could catch glimpses of the water in the distance—of light refracting off waves. In the hosts' home, I encountered Remington sculptures of horses, cowboys, and Native Americans. Wealth and patriotism seemed intertwined. I wondered if, as a minority in America, I would ever be able to feel such a deep openly-expressed love of country.

MASSACHUSETTS

In 1981 during my freshman year of college, while courting an intelligent green-eyed brunette, I was with her at Fanueil Hall Marketplace in Boston. She had already kissed me more than once, but that day a fraternity pledge ran toward us, claiming he had to kiss thirty women for his initiation. Before the young woman I was with could object, the pledge was forcing a kiss. She told him to stop, and when I pushed him away, he glared at me with the hatred of privilege and entitlement, an expression that said he had a right to her, but who did I think I was? Once you have encountered an expression like this, you never forget it.

MICHIGAN

My brother and I met last year in Detroit to watch the Lions play the Vikings because it was supposed to be the quarterback Brett Favre's last game. We were warned by the concierge at our hotel not to walk on the nearby streets at night; Motor City's automobile economy has been ailing, so crime rates are high. I thought of how the American road trip—which I had lived for as a teenager—was becoming a behavior of the past. We lived frivolously back then, as if oil and gasoline were inexhaustible. What is worse? What should remain the same? Still, I hoped for better times for Detroit.

MINNESOTA

For several years I have joked with the African-American poet Sean Hill about flying up and going ice fishing with him in Bemidji, Minnesota. I learned while growing up to ice fish on lakes in the Adirondacks where the ice becomes more than four feet thick. That I could be an Asian-American teaching an African-American how to ice fish in a state first settled by Dakota, Ojibwa, and Ho-Chunk (Winnebago) tribes, with claims of early Norse exploration, yet that was later inhabited by the French, strikes me as a uniquely American occurrence that should be celebrated or mourned with a whiskey flask.

MISSISSIPPI

In August of 2005, Hurricane Katrina destroyed the house of one of my high school classmates, Sue Chamberlain, in Bay Saint Louis. After living in a FEMA trailer, she finally began rebuilding. The majority of insurance companies, however, ruled damages in the town were caused primarily by flooding and not from a hurricane, while almost no one carried flood insurance, so Bay Saint Louis remains like a fragment of what it once was. The first waterfront restaurant, North Beach Food and Spirits, just reopened in 2011. Is six years too long to rebuild? Intending to visit and spend some of my income to support the recovery, I feel guilty for not yet making the trip.

MISSOURI

Once while I was flying, my plane was forced to land in Kansas City due to a raging snowstorm. The slender brunette sitting next to me asked with a smile if I wanted to share a hotel room. I remember checking in, and whatever else occurred is a blur of lost details, like time that never was. We didn't exchange names or telephone numbers, and now I have experienced the phenomenon of straining to recall what happened and knowing what must have, asking, was that really me?

MONTANA

When I flew to Missoula in 2001 to present at a conference, Derick Burleson connected me with the poet Greg Pape who took me fly fishing. Snow and ice covered the river banks, but my eyes detected rainbow trout. Although Greg coaxed some of them to strike with a wet fly, I did not catch a single fish. Since I lived in the crowded city of Houston at the time, I felt utterly grateful just to be outside, hiking through woods besides running water, casting a line, and I felt hopeful for how generously I had been shown the territory by someone I had never met.

NEBRASKA

One notable Chinese-American Nebraskan is Edward Day Cohota, who joined the Union Army in 1864 and fought in the Civil War. He eventually settled at Fort Niobrara near Valentine, Nebraska, marrying a Swedish-American woman and fathering six children. He died in 1935, ninety years after emigrating from Shanghai. Cohota's story reminds me of my paternal grandfather, Frank Gee, who served in the United States Army. Why do the politicians who rail against immigration never mention all the minorities who have served in the military? Too much of politics has always been self-promoting falsehood and manipulation.

NEVADA

In the 1860s Chinese-American laborers built the Central Pacific Railroad, leveling the grade and laying track through the high Sierra Nevada territory. For the last decade Chinese-Americans have been resettling in Las Vegas, their migration fueling ethnic diversity in a city that has long been overwhelmingly white. Ten years ago Las Vegas' Chinatown was less than three blocks long; today it stretches almost four miles along Spring Mountain Boulevard.

NEW HAMPSHIRE

I attended the University of New Hampshire where I was one out of fewer than twenty-five minorities on a campus of over ten thousand students. One weekend, though, during my freshman year, I hitch-hiked from Durham to Woodsville on the Vermont border. John Roy and I arrived at his hometown in the dark. We were welcomed at a bar and everyone treated me like I was family; I drank for free and danced with young white women the entire night. Several told me that they had never seen or spoken with a Chinese-American before meeting me.

NEW JERSEY

Long ago my grandfather invested in a restaurant in New Jersey with two partners but discovered that they weren't paying him his fair share of the profits. He brought the matter to the Gee Family Association, a tong in Chinatown, New York. The tong declared that the two partners had to refund my grandfather's entire investment, and that the two men were never to do business with any of the Gee family again. Eventually I discovered that my grandfather was one of the earliest founders of the tong. At the Gee Family Association building, I was welcomed like a long-lost relative and saw my grandfather's name on a metal plaque at the top of a commemorative wall.

NEW MEXICO

My close friend Renata Golden now lives in Santa Fe. I have been intrigued by how much the city promotes the arts. I also hear that there are Chinese-Mexican fusion restaurants in New Mexico. Frontier Airlines flies from Atlanta to Albuquerque, and then one has to drive to Santa Fe; this is the route I will take to visit Renata.

NEW YORK

I was born in Astoria, Queens and lost what Cantonese I could speak when my family moved to Albany. My parents insisted on my becoming fluent only in English because it was what was needed most to succeed. On April 3, 2009, Jiverly Wong entered the American Civic Association's immigration center in Binghamton where he shot and killed fourteen people, himself included, reportedly because of his feelings of being "disrespected" for his poor English speaking abilities as well as frustration over unemployment. Current immigration detractors overlook New York's Chinatown, a thriving community where immigrants work and pay taxes, and family values are upheld. Detractors focus instead on those like Jiverly Wong and the burden of costs because of illegal immigrants. It's rarely stated that America is historically comprised of immigrants, and that, since only Native Americans can claim that they were here first, my Chinese-America is, in fact, a colonizing American empire.

NORTH CAROLINA

This spring I visited the abstract painter Terrell James on Bald Head Island off the coast near Cape Fear. The island is reached only by ferry boat or private vessel. Electric golf carts are the only means of transportation on the island. This immediately relieves all residents and vacationers of the stress of traffic jams or the fear of serious accidents. I have vowed to return to the island for a working vacation within five years. I was the only Asian adult that weekend on the island, but I did see an adopted Asian child, a girl, with white parents.

NORTH DAKOTA

There is a place in North Dakota called Chinaman Coulee, a valley five hundred and sixty-four meters above sea level in Williams County. I imagine the history of how Chinaman Coulee was named has been buried deeply like a corpse. Chinaman Lake, by the way, can be found in Minnesota; Chinaman's Cove in Montana; and Chinaman's Bluff in New Zealand. So not only are there national racist appellations, but there are global derogatory names that nonetheless reveal Asian mobility.

OHIO

In the early 1990s I veered east to Troy, Ohio to visit an old friend, a Baptist preacher, who asked if I wanted to go sailing on Lake Loramie. Heading north, we stopped and he ran into a gas station and bought cigarettes and beer because he felt free to smoke and drink in front of me, but never his parishioners. That day we hurtled back and forth across the lake with the strongest winds, smoking and drinking like neither of us could ever die. We are both, I'm glad to say, still alive.

OKLAHOMA

I interviewed at Stillwater to teach at Oklahoma State. The eventual hire was the late poet and National Book Award winner, Ai. She described herself as half-Japanese, Choctaw-Chickasaw, Black, Irish, Southern Cheyenne, and Comanche. She had changed her name from Florence Anthony to Ai, which means love in Japanese. Upon hearing she was the hire, I realized the job could never have been mine. I have always associated Oklahoma with humility.

OREGON

An ex-girlfriend from west Texas loves the sun, but now lives in Eugene. I hope she isn't depressed by all the rain. She told me once that every man she had dated married right after breaking up with her. As it turned out, she married the next man she met after dating me. I told her how glad I was to have helped disrupt her unfortunate pattern.

PENNSYLVANIA

When I was twelve our family toured Hershey Park; the factory still allowed people to walk close to the gigantic chocolate-filled vats. Now the tour utilizes glass windows. We ate at an Amish restaurant where all of the dishes were served on heaping platters or in large bowls, and this communal way of dining struck me as similar to how Chinese families share food at banquets, or have *dim sum*, the experience persisting in spite of America's exaggerated emphasis on rugged individuality.

RHODE ISLAND

I have always wanted to write at a place like the Block Island Sound. I hold onto a romanticized image of writing in inspired solitude by the sea, or would love to stay at the Panther Orchard Writers' Retreat in Hopkington, but I am married with two daughters and, placing family first and foremost, won't ever be away from my wife or children.

SOUTH CAROLINA

My Uncle Ed's best friend from the Army, Dave Geyer, lived in Greenville. When my Uncle Ed and Aunty Audrey brought me to the Adirondacks to fish, I fished in a boat with Dave. We all met each spring for over twenty-five years. Dave bought a house on Lake Secession in South Carolina but succumbed to heart failure nine years ago. His widow is selling me his lake house. I drove there last spring with a key she had sent me, which didn't work. Not being able to see the inside of the house was like not being able to see Dave; standing alone at the front door, I felt the echo of a profound sense of loss.

SOUTH DAKOTA

While traveling toward South Dakota, signs advertising Wall Drug materialize hundreds of miles away. During our family's cross country trip of 1972, turning into the Wall Motel parking lot, we were greeted by "Welcome to the Gee family!" in huge block letters on the front sign. My father wondered aloud if they knew we were Chinese, but the front desk clerk didn't show the slightest trace of surprise when we checked in.

TENNESSEE

My wife's grandfather grew up in Kingsport and played quarterback at the University of Tennessee where he was named an All-American. We have never been to Kingsport or Knoxville but would like to make a football pilgrimage. I have wondered if any Chinese-Americans visit the Grand Ole Opry in Nashville. I favor the improvisation of jazz and can't quite see myself becoming a country music fan.

TEXAS

I lived in Houston for a decade and discovered a Gee Family Association and two Chinatowns. I frequented one restaurant, Canton Seafood, and ate *dim sum* at the *My Kahn* each month with Asian friends. Houston is where I learned about the souped-up, ultra-fast aesthetic behind Asian-owned cars called rice rockets, and I watched Yao Ming play center for the Houston Rockets. The city became my second home. I lived with my wife for two years there and knew because of that time that she was the one.

UTAH

My older brother lives in Salt Lake City; to our family's disbelief, during high school, he rejected the Methodist church and became a Mormon. In the 1990s he played a concert at the Mormon Tabernacle. My family was seated beside the Prophet, the Mormon equivalent of the Catholic Pope. My mother insisted that we move closer to the stage because she wanted to see my brother's hands when he played the piano; she was not concerned about our offending the Mormon congregation or the Prophet, prioritizing our Chinese-American family. So we left the Prophet in his row farther back.

VERMONT

I visited a woman in Burlington after having confessed that I had a crush on her. On the first evening we found ourselves in a bar, dancing closer than we had ever been, but when we returned to her house nothing happened, as if the chemistry was missing, or fate deemed we stay apart, so I felt for the remainder of my single days that no matter where one travels, love is never certain.

VIRGINIA

In April, 2007 at Virginia Tech, Seung-Hui Cho, who had been diagnosed with a severe anxiety disorder, killed thirty-two people and wounded twenty-five others before shooting himself. After the tragedy, white people in my small town glanced at me warily, as if I could be capable of murder by association. What was it about America that drove Cho to become a lone gunman? How much was race a factor, in addition to our violent culture?

WASHINGTON

Long ago I flew to Seattle and then drove to Vancouver in a rental car for a date with an old girlfriend who had sent me flirtatious pictures of herself. The drive along Highway 5 was stunning, the views of the Pacific enlivening, like a calling or a temptation. I wanted, indeed, to live on the coast, to always be swimming, surfing, or fishing, but the date turned out disastrously. I live far inland now and sometimes wonder how free we really are to be where we would like. How limited does our own lack of initiative make us?

WEST VIRGINIA

West Virginia has the lowest population of Asian-Americans in the country. In a recent Gallup Poll ranking emotional and physical health and "life evaluation," West Virginia was revealed to be the unhappiest state, scoring lowest. Correlation: not enough Asian-Americans=unhappiness? On October 21st, 2010, John Raese, the West Virginia Republican Senate candidate, was caught on film making fun of Chinese-American Secretary of Energy, Dr. Stephen Chu. Raese claimed he didn't know if Chu's name was Dr. Cho, Dr. Chow, or Dr.

Chow Mein. Perhaps West Virginia shouldn't be a priority to visit, but I'll make my own judgments from being there.

WISCONSIN

One May a group of friends and I convoyed to Madison to run a marathon. On the day of the race the temperature soared into the nineties; none of us hit our desired times. Afterwards we drank beer on the University of Wisconsin's giant patio overlooking Lake Mendota. As I felt the sun on my face and a whisking breeze and shared pitchers with friends, and as the alcohol numbed my sore limbs, there could be no better sense of leisure, my immigrant work ethic completely forgotten.

WYOMING

In September of 1885 in Rock Springs, white miners burned down the Chinese quarter, murdering twenty-eight Chinese. No one was prosecuted; the massacre served as a precedent for further anti-Asian attacks. President Grover Cleveland, though appalled by the violence, later reached the conclusion that because of how anti-Chinese prejudice was so deeply entrenched in the West, and because of how Chinese and American cultures were so different, that the Chinese would never be assimilated. I have crisscrossed the country for desire, love, education, family, work, and to fish, vacation, and explore history, trying to see America for its breadth and its smaller intricacies, never straying toward violence. Remembering the Latinos on the front porch in Iowa, I think of how immigrants are still struggling to be here, hoping for freedom, and wonder, since I have experienced mobility, why shouldn't others?

A ROOM MADE OF WINDOWS

Kate LaDew

HE'S STARTING TO worry now, just a little, that the people he loves most, the ones he can't remember not having, won't be here forever. It isn't a revelation, a brand new, packaged in plastic thought, but it's the most afraid Billy's ever been.

He calls his parents a lot, in class, at lunch, when he gets off work. In the middle of the night, he waits to hear his father's voice on the answering machine, an old hunk of plastic from before Billy was born, a cassette recording everything he says that doesn't matter, strips of his voice looping around themselves.

He writes things down now. He wishes he'd carried a tape recorder when he was little, strapped to his ankle, a wire under his shirt. There's so much his parents have said. Most of what Billy's parents told him dropped like liquid into his memory, colored the ground, and were forgotten. Retracing his steps, Billy catches markings, footprints cool and vivid, but without their luster, like dried blood. His entire mind is a crime scene, clues and evidence, roped off with yellow, and he can't find the little boy he once was to tell him what it means.

Billy asks his parents to call his voicemail and talk, just talk. He's considered buying a machine like theirs, something that won't beep after two minutes. He prompts, says "Remember when" "What happened after" "Why did this."

Billy knows there are things inside, deep, skimming along the surface of his muscles, put there by his parents. There are things he's certain of, like the simple existence of God apart from what books or robed men scared him into believing, the difference between driving lost and driving looking, and what arms feel like after you've climbed a tree. There are things he knows are true but can't quite believe: fish dangling lanterns in the darkest dark, saints healing with their fingertips, a universe that hasn't stopped expanding. His father picking him up, holding him like air, "the sky is a big mirror, reflecting oceans," and Billy still looks for sharks in the sky.

Billy supposes it was early on, before kindergarten and after he could write his name without tracing, that without a doubt he wanted these two people always. His mother washing dishes because his father wanted a country house. His father with his hands under Billy's arms, spinning him like the cartoon whirlwind they'd just seen on TV. Billy is leaning his head back, his hair pressed against his father's chest, the warm, earthy smell that would always make Billy think of him washing over his face like a blanket. Billy's legs are almost parallel to the ground, velcroed shoes strapped soundly, such a kid that he needed a step stool to wash his hands.

His mother calls about a bird outside, bluer than Billy's eyes, and his father looks up, stumbling.

Billy's mother's voice, soft and pure, could always make him stumble. Billy's feet veer towards the ground, ankles scraping the floor and his father's hands drag across him, desperate, leaving bruises on his ribs he'd find days later. Billy is upended and righted in the same motion, his father's knees hitting the floor, arms under his neck and thighs, cradled like the girls in fancy dresses in the black and white movies his mother watches, light and helpless. His father is shaking Billy, breathing his name, and Billy rolls his head towards him, hair spiked across his eyes. His mother is beside them in an instant, a dish-cloth in her hands. "What's all the commotion?" His father tells, in a voice more shaky than he wants, about their little boy and what almost was and his mother moves her hand to her head. "If Jesus came down from heaven," she laughed, "I'd be in the bathroom." Her smile is one of force, so truly meant, its very presence demanding all wrongs to be righted, all disasters avoided, a strength to save and make anything okay again. Billy watches them, the little tears in their mouths, the blinks of their lashes, telling him he was rescued, snatched from harm. He thinks without effort, "They loved me the moment I was alive."

When he thinks about it now he wonders if he made it up, if he was capable of understanding any of it; a kid with carpet burns on his elbows, dinosaur sheets, spiders for pets, but his mother's hands, still wet, firm and insistent under Billy's chin, soap sliding down his collar, his father's weight around him, holding him above the ground like something precious; he understood more then than now, he decides. He knew what he's forgotten.

Billy's still watching his parents, twenty years from when he figured them out. He comes home on weekends and plays the messages, looking for clues. "I remember this" "I never knew" "When did you tell me." He's found his own history project, one that started before he realized and one he won't ever finish. His mother and father smile at him, smile like they always have. His mother is tilting her head back and laughing, soft and pure, and his father looks at Billy like he's out of breath. He makes Billy remember jack-o-lanterns on Halloween, a light in the middle of his father, flickering in his eyes. Billy is more happy now than worried but he knows what he'll lose. What will have existed and disappeared when he can't call and say, "Talk. Just talk." He'll wake up every day with a bright, empty place inside him, like a room made of windows, the curtains from his parents' country house open wide.

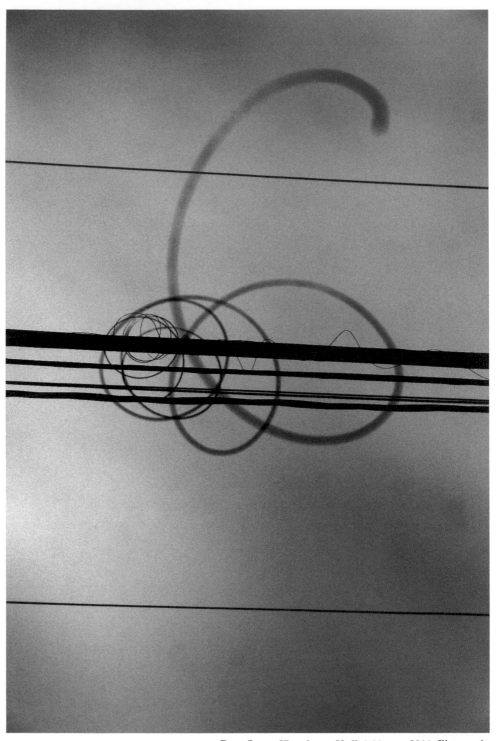

Brett Stout, *View from a Huffy 2:32 a.m.*, 2011. Photgraph.

THE RADIANT

Michael Klein

To go to the Russian baths on a whim—
which is what Matthew and Shane and I just did—
is sort of like getting on the Staten Island Ferry on a whim—
which is what Nina and I once did in my first body's world of
girlfriends and high school voice classes: the terrifying *Carmina
Burana* and then Schubert's haunted song cycle *Winterreise*
and its songs for the haunted postman, the haunted raven.
How did I ever survive my own singing? and still sing—
or did we walk?—the unknown Staten Island until
it came up short at the burned-out house where some clothes
got left and where as a kind of praise to SURVIVE
we took ours off and put some others on that the fire didn't want.
Then we got back on the ferry which in my mind
charged ahead in the story and took 30 years to get to this night's
whim which is the opposite of Staten Island, the opposite of Nina, is
radiant heat or icy water or propelled mint air rolling in steam along
 some classic tiles.

*My mind broke into a hundred images for pleasure until
my body: cave around a stove—was actually there.*

And there again: in the past again but forward, where the poem
 just started—
this time a fallen night's flash in the eye of a sequined hem: I'm next
in line for sex in the 70s: TONIGHT at the Club Baths: drunk probably,
noticeably probably, down to my last admission money loving on
 some weekend
Texan who thinks New York has always been Warhol's city,
Warhol's war cry. OPEN CITY: I tell him. I tell him: wear my body.
I am in the world as object and tonight I meet my body again in the

147

second world of my body: utilitarian and nobody else's.

I am remembering my body in time. It has so many movies in it, so
    many last scenes.

My body has people leaving a theater in it.

My body is of the tribe: not queer, not current, not desirous of anything

except—is this relief?—what comes on by degrees.

I am trying what's left of my health in a certain temperature. And
    trying it again

in another room. Lady Lazarus's heart comes to me suddenly: it
    really goes.

And then, just as suddenly something I would

never say: *I am Radiant. I am in radiant's hand.*

SATURN RETURNS

Michael Klein

Your story about your brother and his image
of God: rubber glitter of what got left when the shavings
from a pencil eraser's drawing of the sun and 10 or so
of its rays were blown away—meant he could see already
the parable of effect as I see it now, finally
after the reading after the lights on
for the reader and down for the listener—myself here
in my fifties after a life of half-remembered music
now listening more closely whenever a story is
this intricate, this beautiful, this fully laid down.
I wish I looked a little better, but my soul has arrived.
At last.

THE POET

Michael Klein

for Mary Ruefle

I'm putting your book by itself so it won't
get mixed in with the usual stuff and the other books I have
to carry around every day like a common laborer
who is always hungry to see something finished and only sees
the empty field with the wind thrown over it, or maybe I've always left
    the game
too early. I can't remember now
what it was I found in a field in Bennington, Vermont
that qualified as being totally mojo enough to be used in a spell to make
another man love me. It didn't even work.
I was dancing then. The whole world was dancing.
Or in love with people who looked like dancers.
And you were there before your book got written.
And this idea to remain anonymous was there, too, abiding us with mercy.
And somebody said: Don't get captured.
And we looked up and said the same thing to what we thought was
    the future
there, with its heartbroken electric eye, filming us from the sky.

THE HOARD

Michael Klein

As if I cared enough about the things of this world and hoarded
some of the gathered and the arbitrary and took them to a place I
called the arbitrarium, there was a drawer of marbles
and string and wrappers and envelopes and
toothpicks, pen knives, pens, loose change,
Tiffany blue boxes, lube, porn—all the crumbs of a
boyhood leading to when I was good, before I got lost and
claimed by the bad. This was before I acquired (is acquired the word?)
    the fire of mind
of me always standing for it. That was youth up in flames
in the rear-view mirror of anything! Poems not just read,
but lived by—seen straight through to the clearer world.
I could feel the obsession of a writer like a heat in the hand.
It doesn't happen anymore: the collection: the gathered or the arbitrary.
I'm the non-collector. Everything I have is already with me,
stained by me: hair and muscle and the ends of sentences inside an old coat,
but still the boy, I think, at silences, who smeared his own shit on the
walls and played helicopter on the edge of a Connecticut roof until
his own brother had to call and drag
him off and made him memorize it: Risk, and the "R" in risk and the "I."
It doesn't really happen anymore, and seems to me all a ruse: the life of
    the mind.
What mind? The one that's left like a shell of the one that escaped at last?
A child looks up and sneers into the thing he is holding in his hand
and shakes it up and down to make sure it has noise and lights up
and moves through his own time like no other time than this one,
like a child God in a suit of bells.
There is no past.
Nobody did anything first.
The child knows a joke he tells to the cynical sun.

CHRISTMAS

Wes Holtermann

MY EX-WIFE DROPPED my son off every other weekend. My son, the blooming fashion designer. He was nine and already the protégé to a mentor who wasn't me. My son was a virtuoso in the realm of the trouser, the mentor had said, and he'd encouraged me to stock his drawers with darning needles and fabric shears, to buy the leg manne-quin, which was now the centerpiece of his room. This, I assumed, was a slippery slope, because one minute he's reinventing the cargo pant all over the legs of the mannequin, breaking at intervals, in the dull moments where inspiration sits limply in its armchair, to work out his math problems for school, and the next minute he's smoking long thin cigarettes, calling me by my first name, asking can he use my credit card number to buy a beaver pelt over the phone. My ex-wife was calm about it at our monthly meeting. "He's becoming outrageous," I said. She made a face like the Guadalupe and said to let him be. "The family unit has exploded to shreds," I told her.

"Hold still," our child said. I wouldn't hold still. I was squirming in his newest work, a hooded, slim-fitting, denim bodysuit. The seams were barbed with pins, and I stood there sparkling, my son weaving around me, hemming me into his Spring Collection. The thing was sewn up from all sides, no buttons or zippers, no apparatus for the ejection of me from the suit. I was encased in denim, and I walked stiffly around the house, carrying and devouring a sloshing bouquet of wine glasses.

"Dad, you have to be photographed," he said, attaching the flash-bulb to my old Nikon. He'd set up a backdrop, a black velour sheet nailed to the wall, and I was supposed to pose there, to look like a Greek god.

My son was having a show at the civic center with models and a glass runway and critics in turtlenecks and tortoiseshell glasses. His collection was laid out on my kitchen table, mostly studded denims and faux furs. Also a series of hats.

My idea of fatherhood had been blown to pieces, but I was trying to salvage it, to adapt my methods to the endowed child. I took him to the horse races, threw money at the window for the horse he'd picked, the one with a French name, a lanky black mare with no chance, and he cheered her on in a voice like Katherine Hepburn. This was a joke. He looked at me like, "Ha! Dad! Katherine Hepburn? One of our most elegant leading ladies?" and I forced something up from my gut to portray laughter.

The show went off without a hitch. Models with beautiful French faces walked up and down the runway, turning viciously. Camera flashes glittered the air. My son was backstage in his small suit, in his horn-rimmed glasses, probably cross-legged in a folding chair. The music he'd picked out throbbed. It felt like blood was being pumped into my head.

I turned to my ex-wife. "It feels like blood is being pumped into my head," I said. "It feels like my head is going to explode blood."

She shrugged.

"All over the walls," I said. "There's going to be blood all over the walls if this song isn't almost over."

My ex-wife was remarkable, I noticed, forty-five to my fifty-three, with blonde hair wrapped in braids around her head and creases around her eyes. Why did I ever leave her, I wondered. Who else would I want to be with? I had dated other people. Alice from the prosthetics warehouse. She was tall and pretty and believed in Bigfoot. I was consumed by the overwhelming urge to make love to my ex-wife. I told her. "Let's go out to my car," I said.

"The show isn't over yet. And no," she said. She seemed sure.

The models sprayed the front rows with their dresses when they turned and people in the audience were writing things down. Maybe small exclamations in French.

"Our child told me he was clinically depressed," my ex-wife whispered. "He said, 'I feel like dying,' and locked himself in the bathroom for three hours. He had the shower radio tuned to some kind of Stravinsky radio event. It was unbearable."

I nodded. "Our son is becoming unbearable."

"He has problems, is what he thinks. He thinks he suffers from depression."

"Big whoop," I said. "Who doesn't?"

A: He's on antidepressants. My ex-wife thinks he should maybe be on more. He's starting to look like Gary Busey. He's starting to get scary. He eats corn products now, is on some corn-only diet. I'm afraid he's going mental. The hats he's designing now are these totally insane, tall architectural marvels. The reviews are off the charts. "A Paris of hats," is what Issey Miyake is saying. I assume he means if they were set up. If the hats were lined up on the streets, posing as the buildings of Paris. Does that make sense? All these fashion people are nuts, the way I see it.

Q: And you feel responsible? For the depression? Do you feel like, as a father, the depression was something that was preventable?

A: I don't know if I even think he's depressed. Dramatic, maybe. Melodramatic, I think, is what he is. I guess there were steps we could have taken. Certain measures. The other day we were in the city just walking around. I went to use the restroom in a hotel and asked him to wait in the lobby. This was the Baltimore with the glass elevators. When I came back, he'd cut swatches off of the hotel furniture, had left chairs with loose, pulpy flaps, strings unraveling, hanging like tendons. That's no way to behave. It was gnarly, the chair carcasses. Luckily there was no one around, so we got the beep out of there.

Q: My sister used to cut off girls' ponytails and braid them into her own hair. She'd come home with about five braids coming out of her head. I remember the other girls' parents would come over for the ponytails, and my sister would have to untangle them from her head and give them back. What they did with the severed ponytails, I can't really imagine.

A: They probably made miniatures. They probably made little statues of what their daughters looked like with hair. As mementos.

Q: And your ex-wife? Where does she fit into all of this, in terms of motherhood? Where does she fit into the emotional state of the child?

A: She has a boyfriend now. He's a butcher at some expensive place downtown. Some place with an Italian name emblazoned across.

He works with big knives, shoving guts into tubes made of other guts. He ties the ends. I think that affects a child. I think there's something about that that affects him. I'm still in love with her. I've thought about breaking his face open. I've walked over to the butcher shop and knelt by his truck with a chef's knife pressed to the tires, but this too had the earmarks of being effective, maybe negatively, on the child's "state."

Q: It does have those kind of earmarks, doesn't it.

A: The family unit has exploded to shreds.

Maybe I'd drunk too many glasses of wine. I'd exceeded my usual eight and found myself freezing in the snow at the doorstep of my ex-wife, having rung the bell, with my hair in wild prairie clumps. The boyfriend answered cordially, smoothed his face into Pleasantly Surprised. "What are you doing here?" he said, his shoulders wedged in the doorframe.

I really didn't know, in all honesty. What I said was, "And you are?" I felt lost there on the stoop. The snow put its arm around my shoulder.

I'd imagined sending the boyfriend away and sitting down in the living room with my ex-wife, as adults, saying, "There are things I want to discuss." Saying, "There are things, I think, that need discussing, regarding the mental state of the child, things which I will enumerate," and I would enumerate them before her eyes, the first thing being the negative effects of having a butcher in the role of "father figure," due to he mutilates animal carcasses etc. etc. etc. saying, "He'll become those kids on the beach shoving driftwood into dead seals, who pull sticks out with intestines hanging wildly from the ends," and my ex-wife would say she hadn't thought of it that way, and, come to think of it, her boyfriend was also inadequate in a number of other important areas and would I like to set fire to his truck and maybe go to the movies? And then it's Christmas, our son weaving velour strips into a loose turtleneck collar on the rug, the tree glittering, spraying the room with lights, the tree which we have personally harvested, as a family, from Ukiah-Dale, a glorious Douglas fir, and my ex-wife is on the couch, coffee in one hand, an issue of *American Bungalow* in the other, her legs draped over my lap, while "White Christmas," in Bing Crosby's voice, rolls around the house.

Yumna Al-Arashi, *Floating*, 2010. Photograph.

ON WRITING
AND WITCHCRAFT

Jenny Boully

WHEN I WAS 13, I was attracted to witchcraft. I wasn't so much inter-ested in the outcomes of the various spells, but rather I was fascinated by the seemingly arcane and beautiful tools of the craft. It seemed to me that witchcraft was like a really serious spa session, not that I had ever been to a spa. (I still have yet to go to a spa.) In movies, you see knives and blood, but in the books that I stole from bookstores when I was younger, there were sea salt and candles, cat's claw and cowslip, mandrake and lovage, rosehips and wormwood, lavender and thistle.

I knew some kids then who really believed that they were witches; I also knew some kids who really believed that they were vampires. The witches were often suicidal, had the scars to prove it, and didn't appear to have any parents. In biology, I cut the foot off of a frog during dissection. I let it dry, and when it was dry enough, I pierced it and hung it from a necklace. The witches thought it was my talisman, and they wanted me to give it up. They met me as I was getting off of a bus and asked to see it. They went through my necklaces one by one and demanded to know which one was the talisman because, they said, they had heard from someone that I had a talisman and, because I was not a witch, I wasn't allowed to have it.

There is a difference between a talisman and an amulet, and although both can be made through witchcraft, my frog leg was neither a talisman nor an amulet. It was just that: a frog leg that had been preserved in formaldehyde and hanging about my neck. But the witches, who never appeared to go to school and, perhaps because of this, didn't know how I might acquire a frog's leg, apparently thought that I had captured and killed a frog to make this talisman.

I wanted to begin, initially, by telling you about a textbook repre-sentative who came by my office one day. He asked what I taught. I said that I taught creative writing. He said that his company had many books to help me teach creative writing. He opened his catalogue and highlighted many handbooks that were written or edited by important writers. These books would help me teach my students the craft of poetry or the craft of writing, and I suddenly realized that, although I had been forced during my undergraduate education to use such hand-books, I have never used or even considered using such a book in my teaching of writing. I politely feigned interest, holding back my horror and shock that such tools, like medieval medicine, were used and still being used to teach writing.

Once, I performed a love spell to get a boy, who I wasn't in love with, to fall in love with me. Unlike most spells in the books, this one only required two ingredients: a pink candle and rose oil. The spell book instructed me to rub the rose oil on the pink candle while envisioning the love this boy and I would share together. I was then to burn the candle for three nights and whenever the candle was burning, I was to keep envisioning this love. I didn't have the rose oil, but I had roses growing outside in my parents' garden; I took the petals and soaked them in water, and I used that water instead. I had many differently colored candles acquired from Wicks and Sticks, a small candle shop chain, where I would also run into and try to evade the witches who thought I had a talisman that I should not have.

Perhaps it was because I used rose water instead of rose oil that I had such a terrible time with this boy. He fell in love with me, and one night, he tried to stab me with a kitchen knife. Like many things, I never told my parents about it. I used to blame the craft: my motives were insincere; the spell soured.

The witchcraft that I read up on was considered white magic. Black magic was dangerous, or so the books said. They talked about the terrible things that might happen to you if you performed black magic, which was usually spells of revenge or spells that would otherwise harm others. The books warned that if you practiced black magic, whatever you did would come back to you three times over. To practice black magic was like making a pact with the darkness in the universe. Some books called this darkness the devil. You should prepare for that.

Coincidence or no: when I was 21, I made a pact with myself: my writing should always be *sincere*.

Although I was horrified by the idea of using a handbook in my writing classes, I thought back to the exercises that I was subjected to as an undergraduate student. Many of them involved thinking about situations and then writing through them. In this way, the exercises resembled therapy: confronting a past experience with the goal of moving beyond that experience to free oneself from buried trauma. The writing handbooks seemed to suggest that one could not be a writer if one had bottled up emotions or had not properly dealt with those emotions. Perhaps this was a direct result of the late 80s and 90s popularizing victimization and placing blame for one's current circumstances on one's childhood or past. Perhaps not. I don't know. I haven't looked at enough writing handbooks to tell if there are shifting pedagogies that mirror popular culture. Many exercises that I remember had to do with envisioning. You had to imagine a scene and then write through it. In this way, the exercises resembled witchcraft; in witchcraft, you imagine to achieve, and it seemed to me that the writing exercises had the identical goal.

Witches are supposed to make an altar in the home. They are to sanctify the altar and keep it sacred by keeping away negative feelings and forces. The goal is to purify.

Today, it's 8 degrees in Chicago. I have left my family and husband to come back to Chicago early so that I can write. This seems puzzling to others. Why subject myself to a harsh Chicago January when I don't start work again until the end of the month?

In witchcraft, there is something called the threefold law. It means that whatever you do has repercussions, and those repercussions will come back to you threefold. So, when, with insincerity, I made that boy fall in love with me, I was returned, threefold, a very bad repercussion.

I know I'm supposed to be talking about the craft of writing in this essay and not the craft of witches, but I feel as if I want to do what it is I'm doing now and suppose that this is really what I'm trying to say about the craft of writing: it isn't about what you are supposed to do but rather what you want to do, and that is why I have such a hard time with those writing manuals.

So how do I craft; how do I write? It depends on what it is that I am writing. My projects are usually long and considered "book-length," which usually means, at least in the poetry world, more than 48 pages. Lewis Carroll said that he believed in periods of great productivity followed by periods of extreme idleness, and I hate to admit that I also operate that way. I may work on a project for three months and then do nothing for another three months. I wait for the moment; I wait for the conditions to be right. I have to be allowed to be quiet, to mentally hibernate, to clear the clutter in my mind. The more I interact with other people, the more rusty and encumbered I become. Calvino said that in order to write, it is necessary to first invent the "I" who is writing. I spend many months inventing this "I." It is a bit like witch-craft: staging a certain sacredness before the sacredness can start.

When I do get to that sacred place, I work daily there. I make myself write a page a day. I regret that I cannot really speak about craft, that is, about the particulars of fleshing out a sentence or a line or revising it to meet my needs. It may seem absurd to say that a certain mystical dream cloud covers my writing time. The time lasts for about an hour. It begins immediately upon my waking up in the morning and, once that cloud has lifted, I find that I can no longer write. I don't force myself, but usually the page has been written before the cloud has lifted.

A talisman will bring things to you, such as power or luck or positive energy or whatever it is that you want to come to you, while an amulet will guard and protect from bad spirits, evil, negative forces, or whatever it is that you don't want to come near you.

I have never wanted to please a reader. In the teaching of writing, I would never ever suggest to my students to think of that most unpleasant of intruders. The reader is the last person I am writing for. I should never want to write for a reader.

The moment that you begin writing for a reader, I do believe, is the moment when you've relinquished your sincerity. The spell sours. The lover who you made love you will come at you with a knife.

Perhaps, in writing, I leave out a simple fact: that the boy that I wanted to love me was embedded within the group of witches and was older than me—18—and also a proclaimed Satanist who had carved pentacles and upside-down crosses into his skin, and I still do not understand why, at 13, I wanted someone who loved the dark to also love me.

In writing, too, the struggle with sincerity and wanting someone to love me. There is a craft in that, I do think: the craft of writing as the craft of getting someone to love me.

I am watching snow blow or else melt into icicles on the various roofs around me. It is 12 degrees. I have no desire to leave my house; I haven't felt like leaving my house in days. I am the happiest I have been in months. I want it to snow or blizzard. I wish it would blizzard for days.

But let's say I'm not writing something very long: let's say that I'm writing a short essay. Then the essay may begin this way: it may begin with a suspicion. I follow that suspicion until it gives me something that I might have been searching for. I let it stay that way all day. I get up. I sit down to write again. I see a hole here or there, and I fill it in. I see a connection here or there, and I make the connection or else try to. I rearrange my block paragraphs. I may write from the middle out or pick up from the end again. I let this go on for days sometimes, but rarely more than that, finding that the intensity loses after too much sitting.

To prepare for a spell, a witch needs to take a bath. She needs to take a bath with water that has been through some process of purification, which can be done through meditation and sea salt. Depending on the type of spell or ritual to be carried out, there are certain oils and herbs that should be in the bath water. During the bath, the witch must, in addition to cleansing her body, cleanse her mind. After this, the witch can then put on her special robe and chant under the moon that is in a particular phase and throw salt and herbs upon the earth. When I was 13, this all sounded like such beautiful fun but I never had the herbs and I never was able to cleanse my mind. I made a very bad witch.

Once, when I was in graduate school, there was a boy that I thought I was in love with, and this boy told me that I had a dark side that he was afraid of and that's why he could not love me.

There are days, like today, when I feel like a very bad writer. I am still terrible at cleansing my mind.

The craft of writing as getting someone to love me despite how dark I might be.

It's difficult to think that it was 20 years ago when I used to think that I could, simply through visualization and the right herbs, get the world to change for me. And that is the worst thing; it's the thing that clutters my mind the most: that there is a 20 years ago and that the world, despite my deepest wantings, will not change for me. And that is the only thing really that I can bring to this craft, however dark it is, to write sincerely because I am dying.

THE ONLY KIND

Evan Rehill

SHE TELLS HIM the only kind of love she's interested in is that smashed glass kind, like with J.C. that afternoon in Seattle when they got drunk and threw all the empty beer bottles out the window of their fifth story apartment, like later when they took off their clothes and threw them out too, and even later when J.C. tried to throw himself out the window, the rain coming down like a veil as she held him on the kitchen floor and he sobbed into her shoulder blade. That kind of love, she tells him, is all she thinks about: her and J.C. and two days they spent in Portland writing bad checks from a purse they'd found on the bus, *This was a different time, you understand, you could still write a check back then without everyone looking at you like you were a goddamned criminal. That's the only kind of love I've got left in me,* she says, *and let's be realistic, because you're a real sweetheart, but when you were going off to prep school in Massachusetts, before you'd started running cross country or had unhooked a girl's bra for the first time, I was shoplifting the aisles of 7-11, or I was living in a basement in Ballard with three drag queens who played cards and drank wine all day, or I was pulling a gun out of the glove compartment of J.C.'s Dodge Dart, his foot to the floor as I released the safety, him yelling, "Get ready, get ready!"*

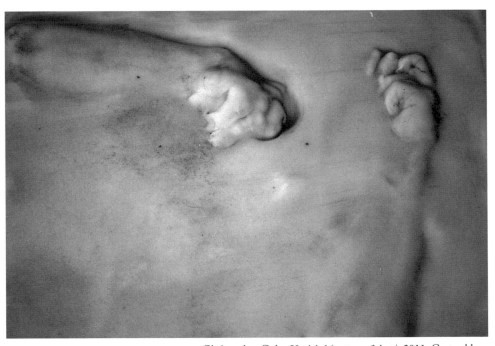

Christopher Cole, *Untitled (gesture of sleep)*, 2011. Cast rubber.

LOVE SONG WITH VEHOPHOBIA

Melissa Crowe

That dream of skulls like eggshells, their terrible
marrow, the vein in your wrist, Kitty, the vein

in your neck, collision of bird and glass and the idea
of your organs, like birds—(some of us are alive now,

Kitty, and some of us are dead)—my uncle's pelvis
puzzled pieces, his chest a sunken steering wheel.

Open rear window: a cousin flying, flown.
I saw him later on a stretcher, like a cat under

blankets, the black bag at his mouth my mother said
would *help*. I remember the day we brought you home,

your father steady at the wheel, but the sun looked
crazy and the other cars full of strangers who couldn't

know how long I'd waited, how your birth split me.
I sat next to your car seat, Kitty, one hand on your

robin's egg head, the other moving over you, not sure
which part to protect. And anyway, apart from

home, where is there to go that's worth the risk?
Not fishing, not shopping, certainly not—*Jesus Christ*—

the airport. My cousin is dead, a little ghost at the foot
of his father's bed, that wheel still pressed into

my uncle's chest, and something presses my chest, too.
The day is bright, Kitty, the house okay. *Let's stay.*

CHANGE

Luiza Flynn-Goodlett

for my brother

The tornado wraps its girth in a coarse
cape of rain, sidles down the city basin,
treads river water. Sirens wail as we pile
into a closet, haul futons against walls.

My mother cradles the youngest on her hip
and jerks us remaining two into a pillowy
corner. Father is a torch-lit blur, both
hands clutching the doorknob. "Hurry up

and wait," he puts it, as we grumble
in the sweaty dark. At dawn, the orchard
is torn, a gap opened like the whistling
one between my front teeth. The barn

has shrugged off half its metal roof, cast
remnants in neighbors' pastures. Even
the magnolia, with the broken door
in its branches that served as a tree fort,

has shed all those cream petals. Yet,
the yard bears no trace, as if the twister
craved a bouquet. We roam flattened
fields, descend the riverbank to finger

the flood, toss sticks into the current
and guess at velocity. Our familiar gone
wild, the day is punctuated by stray dogs,
cow bones, curls of loose barbed wire. Even

we two seem changelings, and we eye our
faces, jumbles of freckles and lashes, mops
of jet hair, for a shift. As though Future blew
in, in resplendent, dark array, betraying

how far we would wander one day.

AN INTERVIEW WITH DOROTHY ALLISON

Marie-Hélène Westgate

I WANTED TO make all sorts of glorious pronouncements to Dorothy Allison on behalf of myself and so many of my peers. I wanted to speak with truth and eloquence about the miraculous effect Dorothy Allison's words have had on us. I wanted to express my gratitude for sharing her work with this new generation of us queer, angry girls who grew up reading books like *Bastard Out of Carolina* alone in our bedrooms all over America and all around the world.

None of us knew each other back then. Wherever we were, we were alone. But when we read Dorothy Allison's stories, we believed her when she told us that if we just survived long enough to get out of wherever it was that we were, we might someday find other queer, angry girls out there in the world: girls who would listen to us, maybe even share some of our opinions. In Dorothy's words, a "nation of outlaws" who might teach us to forgive ourselves for what others had done to us, and teach us to laugh really, really hard.

But I was too nervous to say any of this to Dorothy when we spoke. Instead, I spent my morning meticulously preparing six pages of questions. At noon I drank a glass of gin and called her in California. When she answered the phone, she immediately started telling stories. I fumbled with my questions while she talked about despair and glory. Often we were laughing. I still felt my nerves fray every time I reminded myself that I was in fact talking to the woman whose books I had read as a girl, alone in my room. Mostly though, we laughed, and I just tried to keep up.

DOROTHY ALLISON: Marie, I know this is going to sound absurd but, who am I doing this for and what's it about again?

MARIE-HÉLÈNE WESTGATE: You're doing it for Sarah Lawrence's graduate literary magazine, *LUMINA*, and this isn't about anything in particular. I just want to ask you some questions about writing.

ALLISON: And you want me to tell you cheerful, positive things.

WESTGATE: Yes, and dirty secrets.

ALLISON: Oh god, alright.

WESTGATE: The first thing I wanted to ask is, what do you spend most of your time working on these days?

ALLISON: Fucking mail! It's not even funny, I don't even wanna answer it because every time I answer it eight more letters come, and it's eating me alive. I've been doing this a long time. You would think I'd have answers to every damn question that could possibly be, but no. There are three more people today wanting....

You know what it is? It's all these goddamn blogs. People have so many blogs and, I don't know, I think they put stuff on their Facebook. I wouldn't know because I don't do Facebook. I don't do any social media of any kind because if I did then it would really bury me. But no, it's the mail. It just eats me up. It's more business than you could possibly imagine. People want to become writers because they want to be in a room, alone, quietly thinking. It's like the drum beats of combined media constantly pounding on the door. It's astonishing.

Well, it's the same thing—whether it's mail or email. And then there are all these people who are doing something for school and they want to do interviews via email and I'm like, are you out of your mind? By the time I sit down and answer your email, I could have written four novels. It's just astonishing. And I understand it on some level. I mean, I wrote letters to writers that I liked when I was young. Mostly I didn't get answers. But people who do email expect an answer, and they expect you to deal with long, complicated questions and answer forthrightly, and it's just... it's like being buried alive.

I once wrote Margaret Atwood just because I loved something she had written, and I got a postcard in response. This was about twenty years ago. It was a little form postcard that she had had printed. The card consisted of a list of things that she would get done if she didn't have to answer dumb mail. And I had written her, you know, I love your story, this is the most amazing story… and then I got this little postcard, and when I read this postcard I thought, you know, she's right, she could have written six novels, four poems, and an analysis of Shakespeare if I hadn't been bothering her with my dumb mail. At the time I just thought it was amusing. I no longer think it's amusing. You don't think it's amusing when it literally buries you. You can't get to the important stuff.

And it's heartbreaking because there's a huge percentage of it that comes from young writers who are trying to get published or trying to get a job, and that's heartbreaking. So, does that answer your question?

WESTGATE: Yes, I'm wasting your time.

ALLISON: There's good mail too. You know, where a student you worked with eight years ago is finally getting a novel published or had a huge breakthrough. That's good mail! And you can skim it and send a one-line response. But most of it is long and complicated and involves five more emails.

WESTGATE: Well hopefully this interview is a little bit less of a pain in the ass.

ALLISON: One can be a very cooperative, patient person with a sense of humor, thank God. What do people do who don't have a sense of humor? Jesus. They must take the shine off your teeth, I swear.

WESTGATE: Here's a question about what you wish you were doing right now. If you weren't stuck talking to me, and you could just be alone in a room quietly thinking: do you have any writing rituals?

ALLISON: Yes. Don't turn on the computer—well, there are two computers. One has the wireless broken so you can't get Internet access on it—turn that one on. I turn that one on so that I don't even see the mail. Don't look at the stack of manuscripts in the corner. It's like having to put on blinders. And the most satisfying thing in the world is to get up—get a cup of coffee, put on the blinders, turn on the computer that doesn't talk to the Internet, and go to work. That's wonderful.

And it would be great, if the dog didn't have allergies. And if the teenage boy didn't have various things going on. This is like normal life stuff that interrupts the process. You have your priorities. It's very, very hard to get in place and maintain the writing process. You have to be fairly rude actually, to get to your own work. This is not a problem when you're young and have an inherent supply of rude that will last you a long time, but as you get older and you develop empathy and manners, it's very, very hard to maintain your process.

It's a little bit like, well, I have arthritis and the only way I can avoid being in pain or being semi-crippled is by doing a really rigid routine of stretching and exercise, and writing is like that. You just have to make it holy. And block time out and not give in to all the other things. Let the fuckin' dog scratch.

I try desperately to have a workweek in which that is honored. I try to be as religious about my process as I can: get up, close the door, turn on the computer that doesn't talk to the Internet and get to work. But it's usually only the case that about four mornings out of the week I can really make that happen. This morning I'm taking the dog to the vet or helping my son with some crisis.

And then you have to try to make that period of solid work as extensive as possible. Generally if you can get a good four hours, you're in gravy. I don't know what your writing process is like, but I sink in and go for about four hours, and then usually I need another cup of coffee, or I gotta pee. And that interrupts.

And then there are walks. I discovered a long time ago that there is a certain kind of work that happens when I put my body in motion and allow nothing to interfere with it. Especially when I was younger, I would go walking. I tended to live in cities in which if you walked on the sidewalk and talked out loud people thought you were crazy and stepped out of the way—Brooklyn, DC, Tallahassee. And I would walk and talk, and characters would pop up.

People keep a vast distance when you're walking and talking. And that's been part of my process my whole life. I still try to do it even though at this point I'm supposed to be doing those exercises for my arthritis and for my hips. And talking at home is not as satisfying as talking on the sidewalk and staring at strangers. Especially since my characters like to cuss. There is nothing so satisfying as walking down a street in Brooklyn gesticulating and cussing out loud.

WESTGATE: What has been your greatest obstacle in terms of writing?

ALLISON: Despair! Oh, despair. Losing faith. Losing faith in story. I was a kid for whom books saved my life. The world was, oh honey—the world was pretty bleak. And the place I went to for hope and purpose and meaning were books, novels. They gave me a sense of the value of life. Not much in my world gave me a sense of the value of life.

Even when I was a girl, to be poor in America was to be criminal. And we were poor and we were not respectable. And there was very little to hang on to for hope or purpose. And novels gave me that. Novels were the voice that spoke out of that condition but with meaning and love. Do you know what I'm talking about?

WESTGATE: I do.

ALLISON: Yeah. So I got the notion that that was what it was about, where you could go for worth. And making a loved version of a life otherwise held in contempt by the world—that's the thing that made my life. It's what I go to books for.

I mean, I'm sitting under a shelf right now. On top of it there's *Winter's Bone* by Daniel Woodrell. I loved *Winter's Bone*. I read it and I blurbed it and I loved it. It's about this despised young woman whose family is dirt poor in Missouri on the Missouri-Kentucky border, and she's just barely surviving. And her dream, her idea of heaven, is to join the U.S. Army. Not because of any patriotism, but to live in a world that's organized and clean. Her idea of heaven is a barracks. That vision of someone in such circumstances whose idea of hope and purpose is so narrow and focused and not generally what the world recognizes in any way as admirable just caught me by the throat.

It's so much a reflection of people I knew when I was a girl. Such a reflection of how I grew up. You find one thing and you say,

I could do that. And that was so beautifully realized. But there's a thing that happens and the thing that happens is that the more you write and the more you believe that writing can change the world, and the less the world changes, despair can fall on you. And you can begin to question the purpose of what you're doing. It has nothing to do with what young people think about writing. The criminal thing about going to writing programs and workshops and talking to young writers is that they talk about business. They talk about how much did they get in an advance and an agent. The talk about business is so outside the place where you do the work. And it is so destructive to the work.

Young people talk about money, you know? Like, do I go for a two-book deal or do I want to go for movie rights? Child, you will never finish the book. If you're thinking about movie rights, you're not thinking about the thing that will keep you working. But surviving in this culture... I swear, being a writer is like being poor: the world thinks you're crazy. It's really tricky to maintain your sense of meaning or purpose in the face of all that.

People ask about *Bastard Out of Carolina*. The questions they ask me just break my heart because the questions reveal what works and what doesn't work. And they'll ask me questions about Anney, the mother in the story, and I'll realize that I failed utterly to do what I most wanted to do. My idea was: you would read this book and know from the inside what it feels like to be that mother in that situation. But the questions they ask me reveal to me that most people still hated and feared Anney. They still hold her responsible [for her daughter's abuse] even though she doesn't have the power to protect her own daughter. And that's heartbreaking.

WESTGATE: I was reading the introduction you wrote to the new edition of the short story collection, *Trash*, which was originally published in 1988. You start right off by saying:

The central fact of my life is that I was born in 1949 in Greenville, South Carolina, the bastard daughter of a white woman from a desperately poor family, a girl who had left the seventh grade the year before, worked as a waitress, and was just a month past fifteen when she birthed me. That fact, the inescapable impact of being born in a condition of poverty that this society finds shameful, contemptible, and somehow oddly deserved, has had dominion over me to such an extent that I have spent my life trying to overcome or deny it.

Looking back now, what can you tell me about the effects of "that fact," and the effects of its dominion over you?

ALLISON: You are who you are, and you are who you are by eight years old.

I mean, I'm in my sixties now. I've got a child who's nineteen years old. I watch my son, who is a wonderful boy, and I adore him and all things considered we've done a pretty good job raising him—a bookish boy who wants to be an historian—but he is so much a product of us it's sometimes unsettling. Because he caught something from me: he caught my fear. When you grow up that poor, in the situation where I grew up in which I was afraid all the time, you grow up to be a person who is ashamed and afraid without necessary cause. I don't have to have done something to be afraid or ashamed; I just am. It's just in me.

I recently had a conversation with my doctor about my arthritis. There is this muscle that runs from my neck to my ass and it has been tight since I was three years old. When I get scared enough it tightens up, and it has never let go. It does not let go even in situations when I should feel safe; I never feel safe. And I have discovered that my son has caught it from me. It's like having a disease that you can't cure. It stays with you. It's interesting to watch because I'm old enough now that I see it, but I can't get rid of it; it's there.

It's one of the sources of my occasional bouts of despair because I work with a lot of young people and I see young people who have been shaped by some of the same conditions that made me fearful. There is a balance though because the other side of it—and I know lots of kids like this who've grown up in circumstances in which they felt unsafe all the time, and held in contempt—you grow a muscle. You grow a ruthlessness that is highly defensive. It makes us incredibly productive. It gives us a capacity for working past what most people assume you can do, and in some ways that's really wonderful. It makes us determined and strong and we learn how to use the resources that we have. This thing that we have, it's a balancing point.

Now my son doesn't have all that determination because he's never been afraid the way I was raised to be afraid. So he doesn't have the strength—to grit your teeth and do what you've gotta do anyway. He doesn't have that capacity that comes from enduring horror. He's never had to have that muscle. So it's difficult to talk about, but it stays with you. It doesn't go away. I mean, I used to say it as kind of a joke that some things are lifelong work. It takes your whole life to work around. And I thought that I was being light. I thought that I was sort of joking.

I mean, I know that childhood sexual abuse has so many permutations, so many outcomes in your life that yes, it'll last you your whole life. And you'll have to do a lot of work to find ways for it not to cripple you. But I was always working in the idea that as you get older, and as you spend more and more time being safe and being in a loved community, that in fact you have some recovery. Yes, you have some recovery but you're broken. And you stay broken. And all you do is you find ways to be broken and still be in the world. It's hard to talk about. I have all that stuff. And, thank God, my resilient sense of humor.

WESTGATE: So you carry it with you but it never really goes away?

ALLISON: It gives you purpose. It does truly give you a reason to do things.

WESTGATE: That's an interesting silver lining.

ALLISON: A silver lining on the scar tissue. But, you know, almost every writer that I know has some place of damage from which they derive strength. And I mean even people who grew up happily middle-class in the suburbs. They still have damage from which they derive purpose. It's just the nature of being the kind of human being who pays attention. I think it's something about a certain nervousness. I had cousins who never seemed to register what was happening to them and I thought, there is no nervousness in there at all!

And then I've got friends raised in the gentlest of circumstances whose nerves are so tender and so exposed that they register things on the Richter Scale that other people just don't register at all. It makes writers. You have to have the capacity to pay attention.

WESTGATE: When the prospect of getting your first book, *Trash*, published was on the horizon, do you remember what sort of expectations you had? What did you think might change?

ALLISON: Oh, I remember it well. I was gonna piss some people off. *Trash* got published because I lost my temper. You know the process of writing: you write stories. A collection of stories happens over a period of time, and each story has its own impetus. But to publish a collection requires focus, and you have to approach a publisher. You have to enter into the business world of publishing, and that's a different act than writing. The act of writing is a fever dream. The writing is the impetus either of lust or outrage or desire—all those things that make stories. That's separate from putting together the book and getting it out.

What happened with *Trash* is that a book came out that I really loved called *My Mama's Dead Squirrel* by Mab Segrest. It was a book about stories and humor; in particular about writing in the South. And what the stories were really addressing is that there's a particular kind of Southern story that marries misery and humor in a particular way that is very powerful. And if you grow up in the South you recognize how this is an art form we've created in which we tell terrible stories but they're outrageously funny.

Well, this book came out, and there was a review written by a lesbian professor who writes about literature. It was one of the meanest reviews I've ever read. It was contemptuous of Southerners and it made cheap easy jokes about the women in the book. I read it and became so angry. I can't tell you how angry. I mean, I was kicking chairs, reading out loud, you know—grabbing people, saying, listen to this! I was so mad. And what had happened is that for years I had been publishing my own short stories and an editor had heard me read and asked, do you have a collection? Are you ready to do a collection? I had been so busy, I said, I can't think about that right now.

But then Julia Penelope published that review and I got so angry that I called up this editor and said, let's do a book. Let's do a book that will take the shine off Julia Penelope's teeth. I wanna do a book that will do everything the review talks about but that will be so angry that I will take all this prejudice against us and hit it head on. And that's pretty much what I did. I chose those stories. Most of them are really angry. Even the ones that are about grief are angry. And *Trash* was aimed not just at the one reviewer but at that whole category of people who held people like me and people like the women in *My Mama's Dead Squirrel* in contempt. And there you have it: a collection of short stories designed to give at least one person indigestion.

But I never expected to make any money. I mean, I knew; I had worked in small press publishing for years. I worked for a series of small feminist, lesbian, and gay magazines. I knew because I had learned the hard way and researched it; nobody made any money. Basically this was work you did for love or politics or conviction. So I never expected to sell many books. I never expected to make enough money to pay me for the time spent writing the stories. For a story I published, I was getting twenty bucks. Or eighty-five bucks. Or once, as part of a grant, I got as much as *a hundred and fifty dollars* for a story. It's not enough; you can't live on that. You gotta have a job and you gotta fit your stories in between. So it's not about business. It's about glory. The stories serve a purpose bigger than the twenty bucks. It's not about money. It's not about being in the class system. It's about pissing somebody off, or writing a love letter.

WESTGATE: Was that still true when *Bastard Out of Carolina* came out?

ALLISON: Well, yes, but with one exception. The reason I went to Penguin [with *Bastard*] rather than publishing with Firebrand again [like with *Trash*] is that I had reached the point where I was really broke. I had moved to California to finish *Bastard* and I needed time, and to buy time I needed money. And I did get an advance from Penguin. I got thirty-seven thousand dollars. The book took me three years. I had to split that with an agent and they only pay you half in advance, so in terms of actually being able to live on it, no you can't live on it. You still have to have a job or else you're freelancing; you're living on credit cards. So, no, it wasn't that I was expecting any money or expecting to make a killing. I expected to maybe be able to pay off some credit cards when they paid me the other half of the advance and maybe pay back some of the people who had loaned me money. You're always barely surviving as writers. I know for a fact, you're probably barely surviving.

WESTGATE: It's kind of a miracle.

ALLISON: And then when you start making money, you get in trouble because you don't know how to handle money. The first year when *Bastard* came out, I was like, wow, we have money! I put some money in the bank. But I didn't know about estimated taxes and then there was a flood so I didn't get my mail for four weeks because the mail was held up at the post office because it was unreachable in the floodwaters. And the IRS had taken every dime I got because I hadn't paid estimated taxes because I didn't know I had to pay estimated taxes because I'd never had any money before!

WESTGATE: And you thought you were rich!

ALLISON: For one minute! And then the IRS took the money and I didn't have anything to live on. And I thought, oh dear!

WESTGATE: So then you sold the movie rights?

ALLISON: Yes! Which is why I have a house now. We would never have been able to buy a house except for the cash that came from the movie rights, all of which went into the down payment on buying a house. This is how we survived.

WESTGATE: What was it like, seeing your book turn into a movie? Was that bizarre?

ALLISON: That was very bizarre. Really scary, too, because I did not understand the movie industry and, well, they were all just a little strange. They were a lot strange. Really sweet people, you know, saying really sweet things to you, but they're a different kind of species. They live in a different world and they look at you like you're a bug. And they think you're an admirable bug, shiny and interesting, but they don't think of you as a human being. So it was strange.

I mean, they loved *Bastard*. They would quote lines of the book to me and they would cry. Anjelica Huston wept on my shoulder and kissed me on the mouth, and I was like, well, I'm fucked. But it was such a different world that it didn't even relate to the world I lived in, and I was smart enough to know that I had to keep my distance. And I've since seen other writers who didn't keep their distance and I've seen the damage I managed to escape by avoiding that whole enter- prise. They live in a strange environment and they think differently. It was unsettling. They don't even know they're strange! They think I'm strange. So we regarded each other from mutual positions of oddity. And again, if you've got a sense of humor, it was just hysterical.

And they were ruthless, which is the other part of it. They are very clear about business. Writers—we're bad at business. We're a beautiful group but we're mostly bad at business. But movie people— they're really sharp. They did things that even at the time I knew were nefarious. It was just charming in its way. I can give you an example: when they buy movie rights, they buy the book then they go to write the script. They buy the one book but they read everything that you've written. So when they were doing the script for *Bastard*, particularly at the part when they were in production, Jennifer Jason Leigh [who plays the main character, Bone] read the stories in *Trash* and she would use some of the dialogue from other stories that were not in *Bastard*. Well, they had bought the rights to *Bastard* but they didn't buy *Trash*. *Trash* was the book owned by the small press, it was published by Firebrand. So when I'm dealing with Jennifer Jason Leigh and she's quoting lines to me from the stories, I say, that's not in the novel. She's being very, oh, it doesn't matter.... It matters.

I learned a lot. And I kept my distance as much as possible. And the smartest thing anybody ever said to me was when I was unsure whether to sell the movie rights to *Bastard* because the odds were they would make a semi-pornographic horror show out of it. I was terrified of what could be done with childhood sexual abuse as a visual portrait. I mean, visuals are so much more overwhelming. Things I can do with sentences on a page—when you present a child with a man, it's just got so much connotation, I was terrified.

But a friend said to me, look: you need to write another book. And to write another book you need to get enough money to buy time to write that book. You've already learned this the hard way. They will make the movie because it's now a cultural phenomenon. And if you sign a contract, they'll pay you, and if you don't sign a contract they'll do "Bastard out of Nebraska" and you'll be shit out of luck. And she was right, I've seen it happen enough with other books. She also said that maybe I would have some control but she was wrong about that. But hope springs.

WESTGATE: Did you think about your writing any differently? I mean, once you had a taste of this weird world that opened up after you sold the movie rights to *Bastard*. When you were back to sitting all alone at your desk trying to write something, did you find yourself thinking differently about writing, or did you try to forget all that?

ALLISON: You find you're thinking about things differently, and you fight it off. It's the reason that writers are held in such disrespect in our culture. In order to do what we do we really have to be outside the big culture. We need a lot of information and lot of quiet in order to get ourselves out of that stuff and not worry about the wrong things. You don't wanna be writing a book while thinking about a movie deal. And fortunately, it's so rare that you can fight off that thought fairly easily.

The first novel, even though it takes you a decade, who cares? Nobody's paying any attention to you. Nobody's waiting for you, knocking on the door, calling you, sending you emails. You just take the time you need. And then once you've had a book that's been a success, a publisher wants another book in two years. They want it every other year. That's the model. Look at all the romance and mystery writers, big book writers—every year they write something. And literary writers; we take longer. We can spend three or four years on a book and it can go sour. It's not what publishers want, and that mentality of, Oh my God, they're waiting! Oh my God, I better do what I did—is so Oh my God! It's very damaging. And you have to fight it off.

The thing about novels is that they do take years. The process is going to be complicated; it's emotional. That's just the nature of the thing. Yes, I have fucked up. I could go into church and kneel and pound my head over the altar and say, *bless me for I have sinned, Lord*— take me out of these concerns, take me back to what I really love: story, and strange people on the page.

You have to fight off the world to do the world in your head. You'll screw up. It's the nature of the thing. I find that completely reassuring. The only way to deal with it is to say okay, so, I'll screw up and then I'll go back to work and I'll do what I do. I'll do the best I can and I'll live with what I can do. It's still a hell of a lot better than waitress work.

WESTGATE: Speaking of fucking up, and of scary things…. I've seen you at readings and you're an amazing performer and just as gifted a storyteller live as on the page.

ALLISON: Yeah I should have just become an actress. Unfortunately, I would have had to lose fifty pounds and be a different kind of person, but….

WESTGATE: Was reading in front of an audience ever scary for you or was it something that came naturally?

ALLISON: Who could possibly think it isn't terrifying? The thing I learned early on is that the audience can't tell that you're shitting down your leg. The audience can't tell that in order to walk onstage you had to throw up twice. Well, thank god they can't tell because otherwise it would be really embarrassing. I used to regularly, well—let us just say I had to stop at the bathroom on the way to the stage, and then I learned to always ask for a podium because then I have something to hold on to because I'm shaking so bad. But nobody can tell—this is the part that is just astonishing! I always thought that it was plainly evident so I had to work myself out of my terror. I used to have to take two or three minutes to calm myself down on stage. I had to talk about something extraneous and tell some funny story. Or even say, *you guys have no idea how afraid I am.* But people thought I was joking when I said that because they couldn't see that I was shaking. This is the virtue of wearing loose trousers, I suppose.

But also they just can't tell. I didn't know that for a couple of years. And then a couple of years in, I realized that no matter how horrified I was, how miserable, the audience wasn't registering this. So they would get a little offended when I would talk about being so afraid because they didn't perceive me as being afraid. So I had to stop talking about being afraid and really learn to live with it. What doesn't kill you… will persuade you that you can survive it.

It gets easier with time but it comes back—the sheer terror just comes back. There's just no way around it. Some people take beta-blockers, some people go to drugs. I used to go to scotch but it made my face all pink, so what the fuck. You just have to learn that they can't tell, and that it won't kill you. And once you get past the five or six minutes of sheer misery, it eases off and then you're in the story. One of the reasons I think I can read well is that I go into the story. And then I'm not the person there, standing on the stage, talking. I am in the story. And that's, oh my God, exhilarating. When you're so completely in the story. Mmm.

WESTGATE: Is there a point when you finally forget that you're onstage?

ALLISON: Honey, it's like sex. You become unconscious of the process and it's just a really astonishing exchange. All of you, you and your audience, are in the story. And the best thing, when you're really in the story, is that the response of the audience makes the reading better and deepens your understanding of the story. Sometimes when

I'm having trouble with the story, I'll go and I'll find a place where I can read it and hear how the audience responds and then I can hear what's wrong with the story and fix it. And then I get off the stage and head to a bathroom. You have to find ways to train yourself to see and hear what you don't ordinarily see and hear.

WESTGATE: You've written a lot about the lesbian community and about the South. I was wondering if you could tell me anything about this unique intersection. I haven't read too many books where those two things come together.

ALLISON: I could send you some really fine writers. I think the ones I tend to collect are lesbian and working-class writers. I even collect working-class male writers. I can find a certain lesbian freedom in there. There's a kind of synergy in that outlaw status, which a lot of lesbians share with Southerners and the working-class. Yeah; it's my favorite. These are my people, my tribe, the ones I look for. It's about being held in contempt by the rest of the culture. All of these statuses have that in common, and you develop a certain audacity. Since you're being held in contempt anyway and the standards by which you're being judged are so clearly wrong-headed, then you have to create for yourself your own concept of what is admirable, what is powerful, what's allowed. And that tends to encourage a certain lyrical experimentation. A certain freedom in the creation of characters. It can be wonderful.

You don't even have to be from the South. Make a list of the two dozen best lesbian writers you've ever read and for the most part, what you're looking at is an audacity of language and character and that's what we do in the South a lot. The problem with us as Southerners is that we have a tendency toward anger, in part because it's a cultural artifact. Our sense of humor tends to be a little bit strange.

WESTGATE: When you were a young writer in the 1970s, you were pretty involved with and motivated by the women's movement and feminism. How would you describe your relationship with feminist thought and activism and that community now?

183

ALLISON: Now? Well where do you see it now?

WESTGATE: I'm not sure if I see it in academia or if I see it as a grassroots community, out in the world, with real people. I guess I'm curious because I don't know exactly where to locate that community and I want to know how it infiltrates your life, or if that's a ridiculous question because it infiltrates everything.

ALLISON: The thing I find most tragic working with young writers is that they don't have that sense of community that we had. In terms of my identity as a writer, it was shaped in that broad-based women's movement. And it was an embattled community, broken up into lots of warring tribes.

I meet heterosexual writers who came out of the same small press movements which were entwined with the women's movement, and the heterosexual writers were also very embattled, very much involved in political, reactive, complicated kinds of things. But nobody did it like the lesbians because we were fucking each other and fighting all the time. But we had a sense of meaning and purpose and we ascribed— there was a lot of power, emotionally resonant, almost impossible to talk to people about how much drive it instilled in us as writers. And we did think of ourselves as a nation of writers.

It really was that overwhelming sense of the story shaping the world. It was very, very intoxicating, and it made a lot of literature. You had the drive to be part of that ongoing conversation. It wasn't a conversation; it was a series of arguments. If you listen to early rhythm and blues, a lot of it is someone writing a song and somebody else writing a song to answer that song. Well, that's what happened in the women's movement with literature. Poems would be written then poets would write poems in response to the earlier poems. It was a movement that built on the work, so that you were constantly being stimulated by other people's work and you were responding to it. That's heavy and wonderful and very powerful, when you know that you have an audience.

Even if you don't have readers, you have other writers who are waiting for what you're doing and who are going to write something in response to what you do, which sparks you to go further in your work.

And having that, oh honey, it's like swimming in gravy, it's wonderful. You're just really, really in the middle of something alive and powerful and constantly stimulating. And that's gorgeous.

Now, there is something else that's in play at this point. All these poor little sons of bitches, who write me with little questions to put on their blogs—everybody is in control of the production of their writing. They have their websites and their blogs so in that sense they have recreated that feel of a community engaged in an exchange, but it does not have the power of the institutions who are putting [the writing] in place—magazines, journals, bookstores, community centers, women-only spaces. Thirty years ago, you could go out every night of the week and go hear women read. That's gone. The bookstores are gone. The literary spaces, the majority of them are gone. I find that really tragic, and I find it to be really disheartening for young writers. But the young—and I classify the young not necessarily in physical age but in terms of how they see themselves and how much they've published—those young are creating a whole new system.

I'm going on the Sister Spit tour in April. It's a lesbian performance group that was put together by Michelle Tea [and Sini Anderson] about a decade ago. They got a van and grabbed a bunch of lesbian perfor-mance poets, and they went from town to town putting on perfor-mances and collecting money in a hat and barely getting enough money to buy enough gas to get to the next town. This tour is a month long. I'm just doing two weeks of it. It goes all over the United States and over to Canada. And sometimes they actually put you on a plane! You still have to be a little resilient, you gotta be ready for an audience that might never have heard of you, but that kind of thing is the alternative to what we did thirty years ago. It isn't a political movement though so it doesn't have that sense of sacrifice and purpose. It has literary sacrifice because Christ knows you're gonna be eating rice and beans but writers are used to that kind of thing. To a certain extent, creating a really strong literary voice is about creating a sense of self. And it's odd but a sense of self gets created best in a community—a like-minded commu-nity—that is appreciating what you do, or arguing with what you do.

WESTGATE: A community that's paying attention?

ALLISON: Exactly. I guess usually these days a lot of our activism is in response to the assault of what has become a horrifically conservative nation—the anti-marriage people, the fundamentalists. And then we just develop a short-lived sense of community to fight off those assholes, and that can organize writers.

Writers: let us be clear about writers. I don't care if you go to Sarah Lawrence or Berea College in Kentucky; writers are weirdoes. We are the strange. And we should, in fact, glory in being strange and separate because we are the mirror that reflects this culture back to itself. Of course we're just a little odd; if we weren't odd we wouldn't be doing this shit. We should be proud of being odd. At the end of the day we all just wanna be sitting alone in a room.

Louis Staeble, *Rough Road*, 2011. Digital Photograph.

CONTRIBUTORS

Dorothy Allison is the author of six books of poetry, fiction, and nonfiction. Her short story collection *Trash* (1988) won the Lambda literary awards for Best Small Press Book and Best Lesbian Book. Her bestselling novel *Bastard Out of Carolina* (1992) was a National Book Award finalist. It was later made into a movie by Anjelica Huston. Allison has taught and lectured all over the country. She lives in California with her partner and their son.

Yumna Al-Arashi is a young Arab-American photographer and journalist based in Brooklyn, New York. Her work touches upon the delicate topics of sexuality and politics in both the Middle East and New York.

Hari Malagayo Alluri is a poet, community facilitator, and filmmaker who immigrated to South Vancouver, Coast Salish Territories at the age of 12 and believes in craft and movement. A VONA alum, his poems have appeared or are upcoming in *580 Split, Cutthroat, Kartika Review, Kweli Journal, TAYO*, and several chapbooks and anthologies. Hari's recent collaborations are with Asian Arts Freedom School, Foundation Radio, los migrantes, the National Film Board of Canada, no one is illegal, press release poetry collective, The Purple Thistle, and *RAIN Zine*.

Shayna Batya is a freelance photographer based in Miami. Her work is focused on observing strangers, social issues, and indecisive moments. Shayna's work can be found at www.ShaynaBatya.com.

Eleanor Leonne Bennett is a 15-year-old award winning photographer and artist who has won awards from National Geographic, The World Photography Organisation, Nature's Best Photography, Papworth Trust, Mencap, The Woodland Trust, and Postal Heritage. Her photography has been published in *The Telegraph, The Guardian*, The BBC News Website, and on the cover of books and magazines in the United States and Canada. Her art is globally exhibited, having shown work in London, Paris, Indonesia, Los Angeles, Florida, Washington,

Scotland, Wales, Ireland, Canada, Spain, Germany, Japan, Australia, and at The Environmental Photographer of the Year Exhibition (2011), amongst other locations. She was the only person from the U.K. to have her work displayed in the National Geographic and Airbus global exhibition tour, *See The Bigger Picture*, with the United Nations International Year of Biodiversity 2010.

Lorna Knowles Blake's first collection of poems, *Permanent Address*, won the Richard Snyder Memorial Prize from the Ashland Poetry Press. Poems have appeared recently or are forthcoming in *The Hudson Review, Literary Imagination, The Raintown Review*, and *The Tampa Review*. She has been the recipient of a residency from the Virginia Center for the Creative Arts and a Walter E. Dakin Fellowship from the Sewanee Writers Conference. Currently she teaches creative writing at the 92nd Street Y and serves on the editorial board of *Barrow Street*. She lives in New York City, New Orleans, and Cape Cod.

Celia Bland's poetry and prose has recently appeared in *Poetry International, The Boston Review*, and *Drunken Boat*, and is upcoming in *The Narrative Review* and *The Evergreen Review*. Her essay, "Secret Book Written in the Dirt," will be included in an upcoming collection devoted to the poetry of Jean Valentine (University of Michigan). Her collaboration with visual artist Dianne Kornberg, *Madonna Comix*, will be published in 2012. She is writer-in-residence at Bard College and a graduate of Sarah Lawrence College.

Jenny Boully is the author of *The Body: An Essay, [one love affair]*, The Book of Beginnings and Endings*, and *not merely because of the unknown that was stalking towards them*. Born in Thailand and reared in Texas, she has studied at Hollins University, the University of Notre Dame, and has a Ph.D. in English from the Graduate Center of the City University of New York. She teaches poetry and nonfiction writing at Columbia College Chicago.

Shevaun Brannigan is an MFA candidate at Bennington College. She recently received an honorable mention in *So to Speak's* 2012 poetry contest, judged by Claudia Rankine. At age 22, she was nominated for a Pushcart Prize by *Rattle*. She is also a recipient of an Anne Bartsch Dunne Scholarship from the Arts Club of Washington. Shevaun graduated from University of Maryland and the Jiménez-Porter Writers' House in 2008. She has four guinea pigs.

Ronda Broatch is the author of *Shedding Our Skins* (Finishing Line Press 2008), and *Some Other Eden* (2005). Nominated several times for the Pushcart, Ronda is the recipient of an Artist Trust GAP Grant, and is currently Poetry Editor for *Crab Creek Review*. Her manuscript, *Rib of New Fruit*, has twice been a finalist for the May Swenson poetry award, and poems of hers have appeared in *Atlanta Review, Blackbird, Rattle, RHINO,* and *Quarterly West*. In her spare time Ronda teaches weight-training, Pilates and Silver Sneakers, and spends what time is left behind the lens of her Nikon.

Chloe Caldwell is the author of the essay collection *Legs Get Led Astray*, (Future Tense Books, April 2012). Her essays have appeared or are forthcoming in *Freerange Nonfiction, The Rumpus, The Faster Times, The Nervous Breakdown,* and *The New York Times*. She lives in Hudson, New York. www.ChloeCaldwell.com

Kenneth Calhoun's short fiction has appeared in a number of publications, such as *Tin House, The Paris Review, Fence, Fiction International, Quick Fiction,* and *The Santa Monica Review*. In 2011, his story, *Nightblooming*, was awarded a PEN/O.Henry Prize. He currently chairs the Department of Art and Graphic Design at Lasell College in Newton, Massachusetts.

Susan Calvillo is an MFA candidate at San Francisco State University. Her poems have recently been published or are forthcoming in *Zyzzyva, Nameless Magazine, Compass Rose, Ghost Town, The Davis Poetry Anthology,* and *West Wind Review*. To view more of her work, please visit potentialcadavers@blogspot.com.

Inara Cedrins is an artist, writer, and translator who has taught at the university level in China, Nepal, and Latvia. *Sri Panch* (from her poem's title) was an honorific term to be used only for the king. It was against the law to use it when addressing anyone else.

Christopher Cole (b. 1988) is an artist based in New York City. In 2011, he received his BA in studio arts and Lacanian psychoanalytic theory from Hampshire College in Amherst, Massachusetts. Cole works with sculpture and installation using interdisciplinary media incorporating performance, video, sculpture, and printmaking. Cole has exhibited his work in solo exhibitions at Hampshire College, the University of Massachusetts, and at the Mead Art Museum. In addition, he has also exhibited his work in numerous group shows at Amherst College, Smith College, Carnegie Mellon University, and Columbia College in Chicago among others. In 2010, he was the recipient of the Design, Art, and Technology (DART) Foundation grant, and the Pope Foundation grant.

Will Cordeiro is currently a Ph.D. candidate studying 18th century British literature at Cornell. He has been awarded residencies from the Provincetown Community Compact, Ora Lerman Trust, Risley Residential College, and Petrified Forest National Park. Recent poems are forthcoming in *Fourteen Hills, Broken City, Blueline, Poecology, Requited,* and *The Newtowner.*

Kay Cosgrove's work has appeared in journals such as *Zone 3, Moon Milk Review,* and *Scrambler,* among others. She is a first-year doctoral candidate in the University of Houston's Literature & Creative Writing Program.

Melissa Crowe earned her MFA from Sarah Lawrence and her Ph.D. in English from the University of Georgia. Her work has appeared in *The Atlanta Review, The Crab Orchard Review, Calyx, The Café Review,* and *The Seneca Review.* She teaches American Literature and Creative Writing, and she edits for the *Beloit Poetry Journal.* She lives in Portland, Maine with her husband, Mark, their daughter, Annabelle, and Sophie, the best little dog in the world.

Jessica Cuello is a poet and French teacher in Central NY. Her first chapbook, a biographic poem cycle about the scientist Marie Curie, came out in 2011. New poems are forthcoming in *Tampa Review, Clackamas,* and *The Comstock Review.*

Joey De Jesus received his BA from Oberlin College and is currently pursuing his MFA in poetry at Sarah Lawrence. His video installations, A Hawk and a Broken Home and Hoax appeared in Kinetic//Brim, an event hosted by Harvestworks in New York City (2011). His poem, "Letters from the Athi-Kapiti Plains, Kenya," appeared in *LUMINA* Vol. X.

Juris Edgars lives and works in Ardsley, NY. Mostly he works more than he lives. His previous publications include a handful of poetry in places like *Poets & Artists, The Splinter Generation,* and *Breadcrumb Scabs.* Juris loves Atlanta, and he thinks you would too if you gave it a chance.

Luiza Flynn-Goodlett recently migrated to the San Francisco bay area, after completion of her MFA at The New School. She was awarded the Andrea Klein Willison Prize for Poetry upon graduation from Sarah Lawrence College. Her work has appeared in *Breadcrumb Scabs, OBERON Poetry, Four and Twenty, Ghost Ocean Magazine,* and is forthcoming in *Meridian.* She was chosen as runner-up for the 2011 UNO Writing Contest for Study Abroad. She recently completed her first book, *Congress of Mud.*

Tanya Frank moved from the U.K. to Los Angeles in 2001. She lives with her partner, their two sons, and two rescued mongrels. Tanya has taught creative writing to middle school children and facilitated memoir-writing workshops for elders with moderate cognitive impairment. She is currently attending University of California, Riverside, as an MFA student in creative nonfiction, where she is at work on her second memoir about her life as a parent of a child with a mental illness. Her writing has appeared in *Fiddleback, Connotation Press, WriteGirl Anthology,* and *Los Angeles Family Magazine.*

Seth Fried's short stories have appeared in numerous publications, including *Tin House, One Story, McSweeney's Quarterly Concern, The Kenyon Review, The Missouri Review,* and *Vice,* and have been anthologized in *The Better of McSweeney's, Volume 2* and *The Pushcart Prize XXXV: The Best of the Small Presses.* His debut short story collection, *The Great Frustration,* was published in May 2011 by Soft Skull Press.

Allen Gee is currently an associate professor of English at Georgia College, where he is the Fiction Editor for *Arts & Letters. My Chinese-America: A Meditation on Mobility* is part of a collection in-progress called *Asians in the Library and Other Essays.* His work has appeared in *Gulf Coast, Ploughshares, The Crab Orchard Review,* and elsewhere. He is represented by Gail Hochman at Brant & Hochman.

Kimberly Grey is a poet and a photographer currently living on the South Shore of Long Island. Her poems have appeared or will appear in *The Southern Review, Guernica, Columbia: A Journal of Arts and Literature, TriQuarterly,* and *2011 Best New Poets.* Her photographs have appeared in *The Portland Review, Anti,* and *Two Weeks: An Anthology of Contemporary Poetry.* More of her work can be viewed on her website: www.kimberlyMgrey.com.

Alec Hershman lives in St. Louis where he teaches at St. Louis Community College and at the Center for Humanities at Washington University. Other poems appear in recent issues of *Denver Quarterly, The Journal, Juked, Burnside Review, Sycamore Review, Sixth Finch, The Sugar House Review,* and elsewhere. His chapbook, *Jollyboats,* can be read online for free at *The White Whale Review* (whitewhalereview.com).

Wes Holtermann is from Berkeley, California, where he coaches middle school basketball.

Cathy Park Hong's first book, *Translating Mo'um,* was published in 2002 by Hanging Loose Press. Her second collection, *Dance Dance Revolution,* was chosen for the Barnard Women Poets Prize and was published in 2007 by W.W. Norton. Hong is the recipient of a Fulbright Fellowship, a National Endowment for the Arts Fellowship, the New York

Foundation for the Arts Fellowship, and a Village Voice Fellowship for Minority Reporters. Her poems have appeared in *A Public Space, Poetry, The Paris Review, Conjunctions, McSweeney's, Harvard Review, Boston Review, The Nation, American Letters & Commentary, Denver Quarterly,* and she has reported for the *Village Voice, The Guardian, The New York Times Magazine,* and *Salon.* She teaches at Sarah Lawrence College and Queens College. Her third collection, *Engine Empire,* will be published in May 2012 by W.W. Norton.

Maria Hummel's poetry and prose have appeared recently in *Pushcart Prizes XXXVI, Poetry, Narrative,* and *The Missouri Review.* She is Jones Lecturer at Stanford University and lives in San Francisco with her husband and son.

Michael Klein's poems have been published in *Tin House, Post Road, Ploughshares,* and many other publications. He teaches in the MFA Program at Goddard College and his most recent book is *then, we were still living* (GenPop Books) which was a Lambda Literary Award finalist. He won the award in poetry in 1993 for his first book of poems, *1990.* His new book of poems, *The Talking Day,* will be published by Sibling Rivalry Press in 2013.

Alyse Knorr is the poetry editor of *So to Speak: A Feminist Journal of Language and Art,* based out of George Mason University, where she is pursuing her MFA in poetry and teaching undergraduate English. Alyse's work has appeared or is forthcoming in *RHINO, Salamander, The Minnesota Review, Cold Mountain Review, Weave Magazine,* and the *New Delta Review,* among others.

Kate LaDew is a graduate from the University of North Carolina at Greensboro with a BA in Studio Art. She resides in Graham, North Carolina with her cat, Charlie Chaplin. Kate is currently working on her first novel.

Ann Lauinger's book, *Persuasions of Fall* (University of Utah, 2004), won the Agha Shahid Ali Prize for Poetry. She is a member of the Literature faculty at Sarah Lawrence College.

Christopher Leibow currently lives in Salt Lake City with his cat Mr. President. He is an MFA graduate of Antioch and has been published in numerous journals and online, including *Juked, Interim, Barrow Street,* and *Cricket Online Review.* He is a two-time Pushcart Award nominee and the winner of the Writers@Work Writers Advocate Award in 2008. His images are forthcoming in *491 Magazine* (in the next edition, *Light Feather*).

Christopher Lirette, originally from Chauvin, Louisiana, lives with his wife, Linda, in Newark, New Jersey. His poetry appears in *The Southern Review, PANK, Hayden's Ferry Review,* and *The Colorado Review* and earned him a Fulbright Grant in 2007. He also has an essay on professional wrestling in *The Louisville Review* and one on *The X-Files* in *Pebble Lake Review.* In addition to writing, he has worked as an offshore roustabout, an archery instructor, and a personal chef. During the school year, he commutes to Ithaca, NY to teach courses on poetry, superheroines, and hip-hop.

Naomi Lore is a writer and artist who resides in Brooklyn, NY. She is the Tomaselli award winner for "Best Poet" from her alma mater SUNY New Paltz, where she graduated with a creative writing minor in 2008. Her writing has also appeared in *Bellevue Literary Review, Awakenings Review, 5x5, Naugatuck River Review,* and others, and her manuscript was a finalist for the *Writebloody Publishing 2011* annual call. She grew up in Mamaroneck, NY.

Alex Manthei graduated from Occidental College in Los Angeles with a degree in English and Comparative Literary Studies in the spring of 2010. Raised in Tucson, Arizona, under wide-open desert skies, Manthei now resides within the (slightly colder, slightly grayer) Netherlands, where he attends the University of Amsterdam as a research Master's student. He is a founding member of *thosedamwriters*, an international creative writing collective in Amsterdam. www.alexmanthei.com.

Rick Moody is the author of five novels, three collections of stories, a memoir, and a recently collected volume of essays entitled *On Celestial Music*. He is a music critic at The Rumpus.net and a member of The Wingdale Community Singers. He's at work on a new novel.

Mary Morris is the author of fourteen books: six novels, including *Revenge*, three collections of short stories, and four travel memoirs, including most recently *The River Queen*. Her numerous short stories and articles have appeared in places such as *The Atlantic*, *Ploughshares*, and *Narrative*. The recipient of the Rome Prize in Literature, Morris teaches writing at Sarah Lawrence College. For more information go to her website, www.marymorris.net.

Heather Aimee O'Neill is the Assistant Director of the Sackett Street Writers' Workshop and teaches creative writing at Hunter College. Her work has been published in several literary journals and her poetry collection, *Memory Future*, was selected by Carol Muske-Dukes as the winner of the University of Southern California Gold Line press award and published in 2011. Her novel manuscript, *Hers to Hold*, was recently short-listed for the Faulkner-Wisdom Creative Writing Competition. A freelance writer for various publications, she writes the monthly book column *Across The Page* for MTV's AfterEllen.com. She lives in Brooklyn with her partner and their son. Twitter.com/HeatherAimeeONeill

Peter Orner is the author of three books of fiction, including the recently published *Love and Shame and Love*, a New York Times Editor's Choice Book. He is also the editor of two books of nonfiction, *Underground America* and *Hope Deferred: Narratives of Zimbabwean Lives*. He is on the MFA faculty at San Francisco State.

Leslie Paolucci lives in southern Vermont with her husband and her daughter. She is a graduate of Goddard College with an MFA in Creative Writing. Her poems have appeared in *Cafe Review*, *Thirteenth Moon*, and *Yankee Magazine* and are forthcoming in *Birchsong* and *Clockhouse Review*.

Christopher Phelps studied physics and philosophy at MIT before falling in love with the messenger. By now he works in a small sculpture workshop. His poems appear in magazines including *The Awl, Field, Meridian, The New Republic, Pank,* and in the anthology *Collective Brightness: LGBTIQ Poets on Faith, Religion & Spirituality.* He has no children but a pair of poetry manuscripts, *Cosmosis* and *Word Problems,* looking for homes. Occasionally he writes for the poetry blog www.thethepoetry.com.

Marielle Prince is a native of Durham, North Carolina. Currently working on her MFA at the University of Virginia, she teaches an introductory poetry workshop and is the Poetry Editor of *Meridian.*

Evan Rehill's work has been published in *Open City, American Short Fiction,* and *Little Star.* He teaches at Pratt Institute and Rutgers University.

Michael Sharick is from upstate New York. His first job was picking up rocks. The Robot Holocaust has little to do with Mr. Sharick or his stories, but he is prepared if it should happen.

Louis Staeble resides in Bowling Green, Ohio. His photographs have appeared in a number of literary and art journals such as *Camera Obscura, Subliminal Interiors, Orange Quarterly,* and *Apropos Literary Journal.* His photograph "Industrial Strength Nation" was shown in the 93rd Toledo Area Artists Exhibition.

Charity Stebbins is a recent graduate of the Iowa Writers' Workshop in poetry. Her work has previously appeared in *New American Writing.*

Brett Stout is a 32-year-old punk rock artist and writer living in Myrtle Beach, South Carolina. He is a high school dropout and former construction-worker-turned-college-graduate and paramedic. He creates art while mainly hung-over from a small cramped apartment. He is the owner and operator of the Anti Condo Art group and puts on controversial art projects throughout the southern U.S.

Kevin Strang is an artist/musician from Cleveland, Ohio. Kevin's work spans many mediums and genres. Kevin currently lives in San Francisco. To see more work visit kevinstrang.com.

Elizabeth Tashiro is a poet from Torrance, California. She received her bachelor's degree in psychology and creative writing from the University of Michigan. She currently resides in New York and attends Sarah Lawrence College, where she is pursuing a MFA in Poetry. When she is not reading or writing, Elizabeth climbs mountains, practices yoga, and completes jigsaw puzzles.

Matthew Vollmer is the author of *Future Missionaries of America*, a book of short stories. He is the co-editor, with David Shields, of *Fakes: An Anthology of Pseudo-Interviews, Faux-Lectures, Quasi Letters, and Other Fraudulent Artifacts*, forthcoming from W. W. Norton in 2012. His work has appeared in *The Paris Review, Tin House, VQR, Epoch*, and other literary magazines. He is currently at work on a collection of epitaphs, some of which have appeared in *DIAGRAM, elimae, Carolina Quarterly, Passages North, The Pinch Journal, Phoebe, PANK* (online), and *The Collagist*. He teaches in the MFA program at Virginia Tech.

Kathryn Wiese studies creative nonfiction at Lesley University in Cambridge, Massachusetts. The essay "Twenty Miles from Wisdom" is the first chapter of her yet-to-be published book of the same title.

Anne-E. Wood's work has appeared in *Tin House, New Letters, AGNI, The Chicago Quarterly Review*, and others. She teaches writing at Rutgers University and Gotham Writers' Workshop. She lives in Brooklyn and is at work on a novel.

Christopher Woods is a writer, teacher, and photographer who lives in Texas. His books include a prose collection, *Under A Riverbed Sky*, and a book of stage monologues for actors, *Heart Speak*. His photo essays have appeared in *Public Republic, Deep South, Glasgow Review*, and *Narrative Magazine*.

Marie-Hélène Westgate is a recent graduate of Sarah Lawrence College's MFA program in nonfiction and is currently at work on a novel. She lives with her partner in Brooklyn where she spends as much time as possible locked alone in a room, quietly thinking.